The Works of Michael Ryan Architects

UN EXP ECT

Written by Michael Ryan
Introduction by Gray Read
Edited by 160over90

OSCAR RIERA OJEDA
PUBLISHERS

ACKNOWLEDGEMENTS

160OVER90

Five years ago, in 2007, I received a call from Darryl Cilli. He wanted to renovate his house in a suburb near Philadelphia. The house was a generic 1970s builder's model. He and his wife, Anne, wanted to stay in their community and decided that re-thinking the spaces and the architecture would suit their needs for many years. Darryl is Chief Creative Officer and Principal of 160over90, an advertising and branding agency based in Philadelphia. He seemed to have a keen interest in design and had researched numerous architects for the project.

We discussed his goals and then agreed that the budget and his expectations did not match.
He accepted this with a rare sense of realism. Months later, I received my second call from Darryl. The project could now move forward and our work together transformed the home.

Just before the holidays in 2010, Darryl invited me to his office with a proposal. He suggested that MRA be a special project for the agency. He outlined a process, with the tangible goals being a new website and ultimately, a monograph. We decided to proceed. There was an initial process of discovery during which his project team interviewed clients, contractors, and craftspeople. They travelled to visit a series of completed projects. At the same time, we worked to assemble 22 years of "assets," as the team referred to them: photography, drawings, and models. The team at 160over90 created a framework and outlined goals for our year ahead.

Assembling a book that would reflect my work was not a new idea for me. The interest was always there, but the pull required to draw my focus away from current projects was not. Making the commitment to work with a group of talented people changed this feeling. Megan Pomplas and Cory McCall managed the process and the creativity. They pushed us when necessary but also allowed us slack to consider the content when we needed a break. Following their interviews and project visits, they understood the underlying philosophy of the firm; Cory would give the book its title. Bradley Fallor edited my writing, formatting and refined the words in order to tell a story. Kelly Dorsey sifted through our office one day when I was not there, taking pictures of random ephemera. We can blame Kelly for the picture you'll see when you turn the page, an old polaroid among many sitting behind my monitor. Justin LaFontaine was there early for the discovery; the fun part. He re-joined at a crucial time to design the monograph, assembling the ideas outlined in the creative brief; formatting the various chapters and projects. He worked magic with certain images, forcing us to look at them in a new way.

THE BOOK

I was open to the idea of a book that wandered from more typical monographs. We all agreed that the book should reach an audience of clients and enthusiasts, as well as architects and designers. Works would be presented in a clear way, with photography at a scale that would invite the viewer. The primary projects, of which there are six, were selected to showcase the diversity of the work and how it relates to the particular circumstances of a specific building. In this case, we selected single houses as a framework for sharing our work.

One of the written assignments from 160over90 consisted of describing the projects' backstories. I ran on and on and the projects seemed to take their realized shape from the stories and circumstances that surrounded their creation. The stories became the projects' objectivity and the architecture shifted to something much more subjective; something personal. It was important to me that the projects selected for this book reveal this.

I approached Gray Read, a friend, and professor of Architectural Theory at Florida International University, about writing an introduction for the book. Gray and I had been classmates in graduate school at the University of Pennsylvania. She had pursued an academic career while mine focused solely on practice. Despite this, we had remained in contact and I had followed her published work, enjoying her views on buildings and places, as well as her sense of humor and candor. She agreed to take on the intro; reviewed the work and intentions for the book; and, in essence, delivered a backstory.

WE WORK TOGETHER

Architects are acutely aware that the pursuit is collaborative. It's impossible to look at the projects in this book without thinking of my collaborators. I have been fortunate to work alongside many excellent architects. Their names are listed in the project credits but their work permeates every page.

Rich Villa and I have been working together for fourteen years. His work is unbridled, unedited, and impulsive. That's a compliment. He is constantly looking to something new and views design as an act of making a "proposition"; something to consider.

Sam Kim arrived at MRA three months after Rich. His work is matched with his ability to communicate and engage with people, without frustration or conflict. Sam's hand and refined aesthetic are responsible for the architectural drawings that begin on page 204. He managed the process with 160over90 and was invaluable in the making of this book.

We work together, my wife Randee and I. As her interior design work complements and extends the architecture, she helped shaped this book in significant ways, adjusting the tone as well as the size. It is an architect's impulse to make a small book, in the hopes of being taken seriously. Randee felt that we should let people into the works, in a manner consistent with the presentation of many large, full images. Randee was right. She has been my editor throughout the process, shaping the text; redirecting my view.

It is to Randee that I dedicate this book.

Overthinking can be bad.

Overknowing can be worse.

LOVELADIES HARBOR SALES OFFICE soon after completion in 1954.
Sydney Shelov, Architect. Michael Ryan Architects' Long Beach Island NJ office, established 1989.

Contents

Draw like a bandit. Think like a gibbon.

Essay by Gray Read

At The University of Pennsylvania Mike and I were classmates and friends. We had a studio class taught by Aldo van Eyck, a playful Dutch populist, who had asked us to design spaces for wild animals in the city.

Van Eyck challenged us to think from the point of view of the animal, to imagine ourselves as a creature that experienced the world with different eyes and a different body. We could choose a giraffe, a hippo, or a gibbon. Through that semester, the world slowly shifted, so we no longer looked at it from the outside—as an architectural drawing—but began to dwell within it and see it newly by conjuring ourselves as another being.

At the end of the term, in the tradition of architecture students, we worked day and night to finish our projects for the final presentation. A small group of us saved the last night to create big drawings on oversized paper of a giraffe, a hippo, and a gibbon to appear at the entry of the building when Van Eyck arrived in the morning. We worked all night on the magic trick. Mike's gibbon glowed with many colors of pastel smoothed together to give the limbs roundness and texture. It had muscular legs, sinewy arms, and long fingers, so it seemed ready to jump off the page and run around the campus. The gibbon, with the hippo and giraffe, greeted everyone who came in that day to attend the very serious final reviews of the student work. Van Eyck smiled.

During our last year at Penn, I arrived at school on Valentine's Day to see a huge, cardboard heart somehow strapped to the top of the building. It said: RANDEE, I LOVE YOU. I don't know how Mike got up there or how he rigged it to stay put in the winter breeze, but Randee got the message and they have loved and supported each other ever since. At that time Randee worked for a theater company, and even now I see her sense of setting the stage for the events of daily life in the interiors she creates for their projects today. Randee is a master shopper, who can choose the best of things on the market, and Mike is a designer to his soul, who can create unique things from simple materials. In the balance of those two skills the architecture firm reflects their partnership in love and life.

Mike still has the gibbon in him, and it sometimes pops out to play. I think it reminds him to see things for what they are and to have fun. He says that each project is a discovery, so each one holds a surprise and some new view, perhaps of a familiar situation seen differently.

"We graduated from Penn as energetic, young architects in the middle of a recession. There were no jobs to be had, and we still needed to learn the nitty gritty, day-to-day tasks of a professional."

By the time he came to the University of Pennsylvania for graduate school, Mike could draw like a bandit and would try anything. Mike had come from Penn State, where he studied architecture as an undergrad in an environment of both camaraderie and do-it-yourself conviction. The design studio and wood shop were the center of life for students who drew by the yard and built things by hand. Experimentation was welcome.

The central tradition that we shared as students at Penn came from Louis Kahn, the great architect who had taught for many years in the school, leaving an intellectual legacy that shaped much of our education. Kahn's approach to design is often reduced to a series of aphorisms: "Build the ruin first," "The structure makes the light," "Ask the brick what it wants to be." Each is a rather clumsy poke into a rich and nuanced approach to the discipline of architecture that continues to guide the best of contemporary work. At the center is hard work and respect: for the environment, for the people who will inhabit the places architects create, and for the materials and craftsmanship that go into building. Kahn designed for light and for conversation—both ephemeral qualities, one natural and the other human, that can be shaped but not determined by architecture.

When you look at the projects shown here, notice also how each of the materials—stone, wood, and glass—shows its distinct character. They reveal their natural origins in their weight, scale, color, and grain, so stone is clearly stone and wood is wood. Mike once ordered tile for a small beach house, then realized, when the shipment arrived, that the tiles were too big for the scale of the house. So he broke them. A sharp hammer blow to the center broke each one into radiating shards that were then grouted in place to make a pattern like rain jumping on the surface of water. It was beautiful and unexpected. Like the gibbon.

Mike and I share an interest in vernacular architecture, particularly houses that have adapted over time to the conditions of the places they inhabit and to the culture of the people who inhabit them. At Penn, he chose to design housing for his final thesis project and did studies of dense neighborhoods in Japan. He found an orderly (even mathematical) spatial complexity in the three-dimensional patterns of indoor and outdoor spaces, so that each important room opens to a courtyard or roof deck or even to an outdoor space underneath a raised room. I remember a plaster cast he made of his design project that was rough and hand-made looking (I think his first casting broke), but the spatial patterns of interconnecting spaces in three dimensions leapt out as a composition. Small slanted roofs popped up out of an almost-grid of elements at varying levels so indoor and outdoor spaces were interlinked.

For reasons I never understood, the faculty reviewers did not love the project. However, it revealed Mike's fascination with three-dimensional composition, and with the experience of moving up into a living space, then out to find an outdoor perch where one can look back through the building and out over the landscape. In many of his houses, you can do just that.

We graduated from Penn as energetic, young architects in the middle of a recession, so there were no jobs to be had, and we still needed to learn the nitty-gritty, day-to-day tasks of a professional. We both wound up in the same struggling office, where we drew window details and ran diazo prints of large hand drawings. Mike understood better than I that you have to start at the bottom, so he resolved to run the best damn prints he could, then draw good details, then see to it that they fit together.

After a year or so, Mike realized that if he wanted to really design buildings that he would have to go where buildings were being built. The economy was still weak, so very little construction was going on in Philadelphia—yet, paradoxically, beach houses were in demand along the Jersey shore. Like an echo of the building boom in Miami Beach during the Great Depression, the shore needed architects, so Mike went. It was a good move. They say that one can only master an art after at least 10,000 concentrated hours of practice. Mike found his 10,000 hours designing beach houses.

Mike would take me on a tour of his houses, many of them on Long Beach Island, like a gallery walk, but by car. I saw many houses still under construction, so we would walk up through the bones of the structure and feel the spaces unfolding, half in reality and half still in the imagination, while Mike explained the ideas behind the designs. The tour was like a collection of stories, each with a specific place and specific people, and Mike wove the plot—in the sense of a design idea that became clearer as it developed.

Most of the shore houses were raised on pilings so I recognized the shady place underneath for kickball, cars, and neighborly conversation from vernacular houses. Also from the vernacular came the light frame walls with windows placed almost casually, as if they might

"The spatial patterns of interconnecting spaces in three dimensions leapt out as a composition."

"Small slanted roofs popped up out of an almost-grid of elements at varying levels so indoor and outdoor spaces were interlinked."

move around seeking a view. In all Mike's houses, the windows are placed so you can see clean through to the other side. The rooms seem airy because they are. One can feel comfortable with natural ventilation deep into the summer.

I'll offer two details from the many that stick out as pictures in my mind. In one house, Mike placed a window immediately beside a bathroom mirror, so while you see yourself shaving or brushing your hair, your eyes might slip across a thin mullion to a long view toward the sea—equally framed so the two views became partners. I'm sure there is something deeply philosophical about that (or not), but that's for the family who lives there to ponder. The second detail is a slit along the top of a vaulted ceiling that lets the sunlight appear as an elusive glowing stripe on the floor—so simple, so cosmological—the passage of the sun ruling the day at the beach.

Mike is a true architect. He and Randee are back in Philadelphia now, and the firm has a broad palette of projects that spans from residential to commercial and institutional work, building carefully toward larger projects. When Mike's ideas rise out of the ground in construction, like the prolific number of projects he shows here, they are tempered in the discipline of craftsmanship. He knows how to build, so that his buildings age well, as architecture should.

First because they are well thought out in the playful spirit of a practical architect, so people love them and live well with them. The real test of durability is less in rigidity than in grace. Second, the buildings are not fussy or obsessively specific, so they are comfortable to inhabit, come who may. And third, they weather well. Louis Kahn spoke of distinguishing the permanent parts of a building such as structure from the impermanent parts, such as windows and interior walls, which may be replaced over time. Mike similarly thinks ahead into the processes of weathering, reuse, and rebuilding, so his structures become part of a landscape that inevitably changes over time.

As has our friendship. When I saw Mike and Randee to talk about writing this piece, we mused on our own aging, and laughed over how our roles have changed since we drew with chalk on big paper just for fun. The conversation rolled and roiled as we leaned back, looked out the window, remembered things forgotten and speculated on things unseen. Of course the setting for talk was excellent, with good light and a view out, like so many of the places he has designed. When you look at the projects shown in this monograph, notice how the light enters and the view reaches out, and imagine having a conversation there.

MICHAEL
RYAN
ARCHITECTS
LOVELADIES HARBOR

Contemporary culture places an unfortunate emphasis on "knowing what you want" and, of course, "being smart." Unfortunately this works against the design process.

Many clients bring this to the table, and it can hinder discovery and surprise. It is crucial when designing a home that our clients have an open mind with regard to the process. It's all about letting go.

This goes for the architect as well. We need to act as receivers, open to everything that surrounds the making of a building. For us, openness is the ultimate virtue, just one step above optimism.

I work toward an understanding of the potential that really exists, filtering reality from fantasy; and, alternately, creating fantasy from reality.

It is impossible to conjure a building from knowledge only.

You need to let go.

LET GO. Ring buoy, vinyl letters. 20-inch diameter.
Joe Begonia, artist, friend, & client.

Our story begins thirty years after our story begins.

It was the fall of 1997. Randee and I had just returned home from a trip to Scotland. This was the era just before we all started bowing at the feet of the all-encompassing email, smartphone, and social media. This was when getting away meant something different. Although it felt good to be home, I had a feeling that the office was in need of a new project. Things had been slow over the summer.

I have always had two alternating emotions regarding the flow of work in the firm: too busy or too slow. This is a consistent state of mind among all architects. It has always been important for me to have a busy office. The work is better, like good service in a busy restaurant. With too much time, things become overwrought and too precious, setting the stage for disappointment.

This was also the era when we taped our phone messages to the double doors that lead back to Randee's office, the conference room, and my studio. Upon our return, we discovered a layered bundle of at least fifteen sheets affixed to the glass. Yanking them down, I quickly glanced through them to see if there was anything promising. And there it was.

The note referred to a specific property and the desire to construct a new home. According to the note's taker, the potential clients had seen a number of our houses and were anxious to discuss the possibilities for this oceanfront site in Loveladies.

It was hard to believe that my history with this particular property began 15 years earlier. Now it was coming full circle.

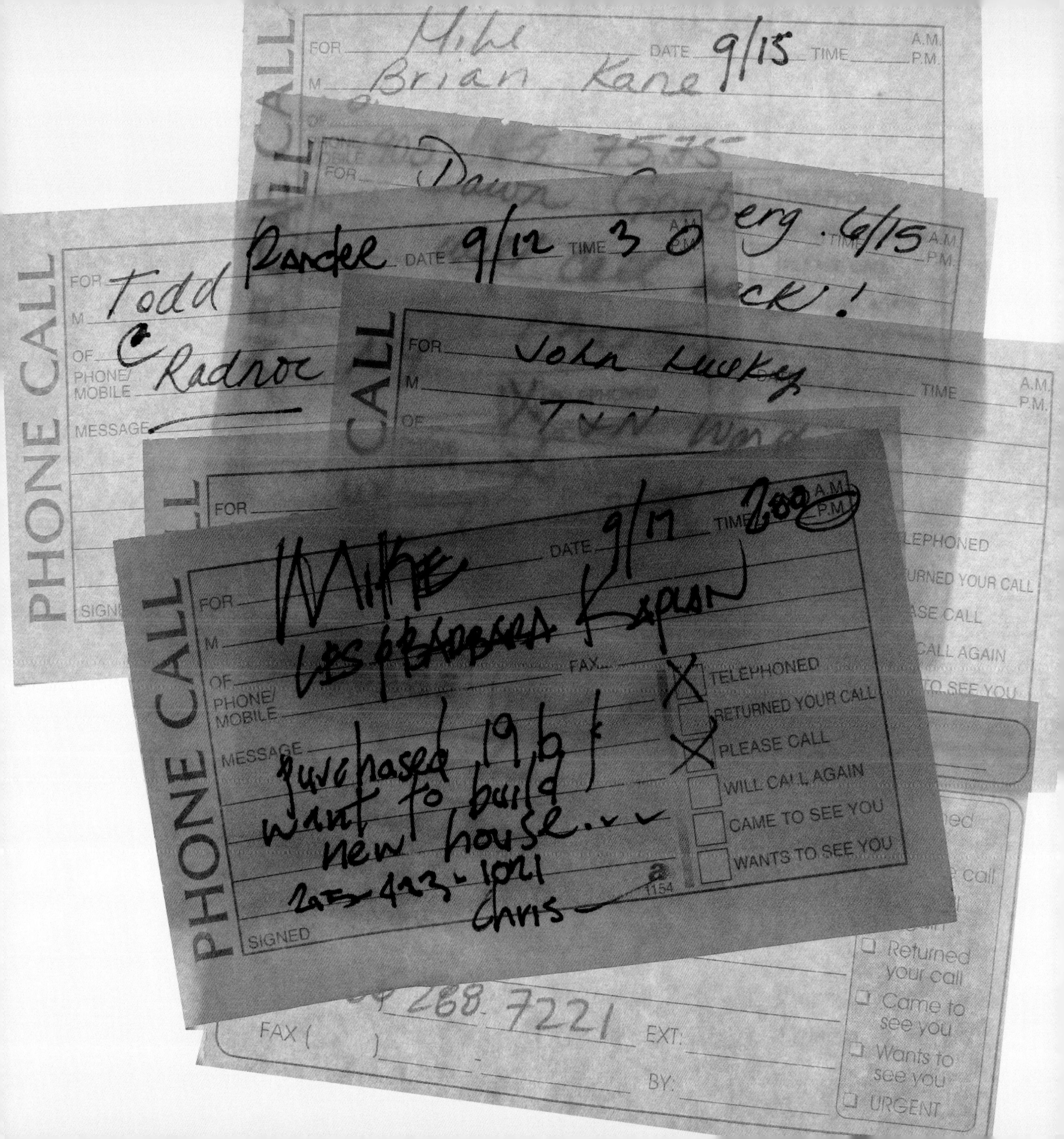
PHONE CALL
FOR Mike
DATE 9/17
TIME 2:00 P.M.
M LES & BARBARA Kaplan
PHONE/ MOBILE
MESSAGE purchased 19 1/2 ac!
want to build
new house...
Chris
TELEPHONED
RETURNED YOUR CALL
PLEASE CALL
WILL CALL AGAIN
CAME TO SEE YOU
WANTS TO SEE YOU
SIGNED
FOR Todd
OF Radnor
FOR John Luckey
FOR Mike
DATE 9/15
M Brian Kane
FAX
EXT.
BY:
Returned your call
Came to see you
Wants to see you
URGENT

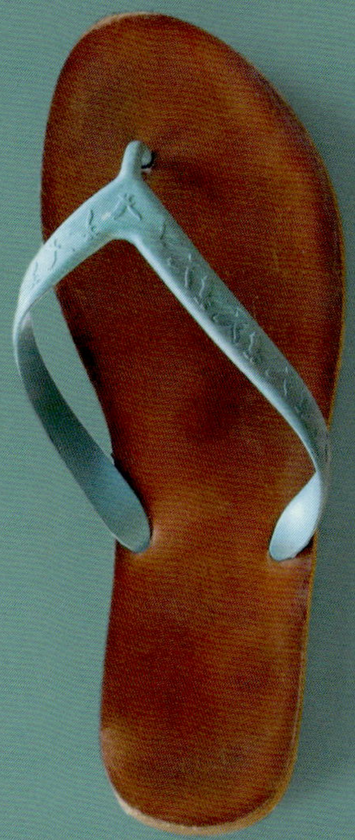

BEACH FLOP

My serendipitous history with the property in question began in the summer of 1981. Our good friend had been working for an architect on Long Beach Island NJ, and indicated that the firm needed another intern. He persuaded us to visit LBI and consider a move. The three of us arranged to meet at the lot that would affect so much of our future — an oceanfront property— to view a new house that was nearing completion in a town called Loveladies. Randee and I had never visited the area before.

In 1981, many of the tracts on Loveladies were not subdivided. Houses sat back from the road on casual dirt lanes. Driving off the road, up a small gravel lane through wild bayberry and pine trees, the new house appeared. Formally speaking, it was modern, but the material was the traditional wooden shingles of older beach houses. The shingles allowed the crisp volumes to appear like a skin. They were new and were the color of light honey. The air had a fresh-sawn fragrance mixed with a familiar smell, like a surf shop.

There was a history of experimental design on LBI with houses by Robert Venturi in Barnegat Light, and works by Richard Wurman and David Beck of Philadelphia. They seemed to grow from the social revolution of the previous decades. They were using traditional materials to create modern forms and spaces that responded to their environment.

Moreover, people were looking for a more individual approach to creating their second home. There was a demand for design. There was good work being created under casual circumstances without stylistic or contextual constraint. And there was the strong temptation of working in this type of environment—hands-on, with clients relaxed about issues of style, not to mention the attractive prospect of seeing my work completed and built.

Chris Jeffrey photographs, in situ, the model he constructed.

Step one:
Knock your house down

Before we get to that fateful sticky note in 1997, we have to make a quick stop in 1995.

My own practice is up and running, just down the road from the very house that drew me to Loveladies in the first place. The firm wasn't the only thing that had grown. In fifteen years, the dune near that house had risen a good three to four feet higher, so it now looked small and a bit dug in.

Different owners had since purchased the house, and they wanted to add to the original in a significant way. We completed the design and construction began. And then, a rare occurrence: the project is halted, half finished, and the house sits, open and at the mercy of the weather.

Now, two years and one phone message later, the property has new owners yet again. They were not the first to consider the fate of the house and its half-finished sibling. The property alone was quite large, consisting of three standard building lots. In a sense, it was also quite rare, since most parcels on Long Beach Island had long been subdivided. Throughout that entire summer, I had been asked to accompany realtors with their prospective buyers and offer my take on the project.

There was just one problem. Because of the half-finished structure's long exposure to the elements, I explained, it would have to be demolished. Entirely.

"Two days and the lot will be clean," I would say. The prospective buyers were always puzzled by this news. For many, it was—quite literally—a deal breaker. They simply could not accept the notion that they would have to start from scratch.

But the new owners didn't balk at demolition. They had the rare ability to look beyond what was right in front of their eyes.

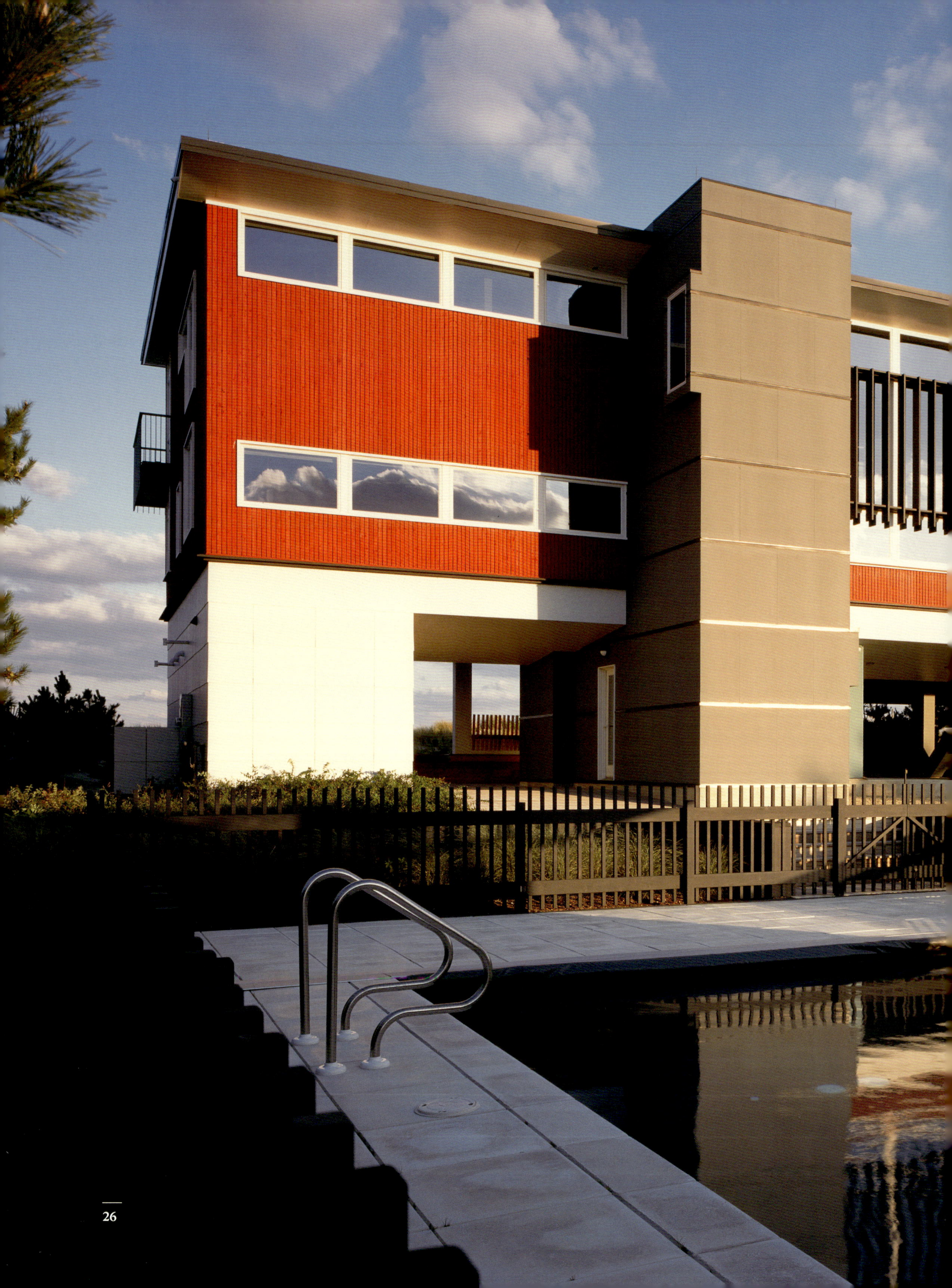

We often prefer temporal materials that weather with time. They give the houses a comfortable lived-in feel, and also acknowledge the generations who live in and pass through them.

Finding an elegant way to flop

Now faced with nothing but sand and three empty lots, we got to work. The clients' goal was to create, in their own words, a "beach flop"—a summer place for their family and friends to relax in. They also looked forward to the new friendships that would occur by creating this place.

It should be open and fun, they said. Not too large, with small bedrooms and closets just large enough for weekend guests. And no garage, either—just covered parking and a little storage for beach gear. This was to be a place where you should feel welcome, just as long as you didn't overstay.

This is an example of how a project, while being fully developed throughout, is often about a couple of memorable spaces. One is somewhat residual or leftover, while the other is a primary gathering space connected to the surrounding environment. The important spaces were to be the shared spaces. Living areas with an open kitchen. A screen porch as a place to enjoy the summer breezes.

We would raise the house up in a way that would be elegant, allowing an unbroken view of the dune and sky as one approaches. This space would be for shaded parking and hosing off beach toys and people. Each step in the design process would result in the house becoming smaller and narrower, equalizing the ocean views with those of the pool area and bay.

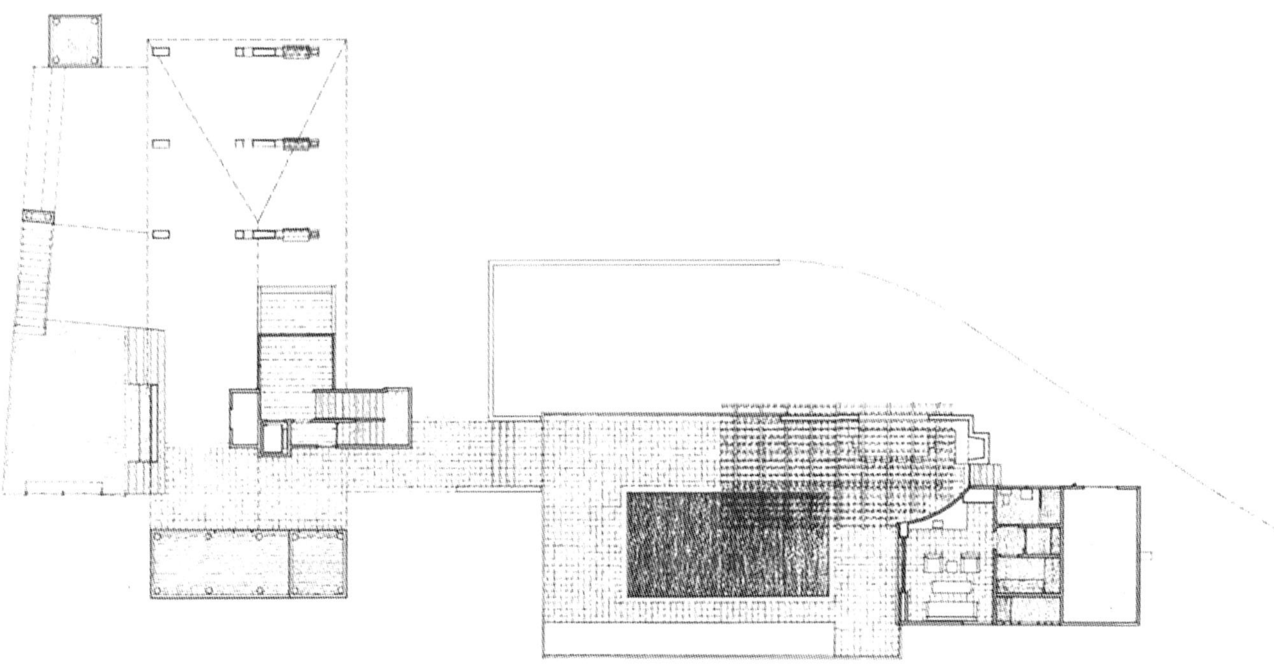

A plan of the ground level

I felt it was critical to place the living areas on the first level above grade. With a building height limit restricted to 32 feet starting at the roof, we dedicated all of the residual height to the open space beneath the house.

Beneath the "belly" of the house, guests encounter unobstructed views of the dune and sky. Greeting them is an unexpected, elegant entrance made of wood and glass.

We can't lose sight of the fact that, ultimately, this place was built for a family to build memories.

The living area emphasizes an openness to welcome and entertain visitors. Whether in bright, natural light or in front of the fireplace, the area conveys figurative and literal warmth.

left exposed and the house on top, they appear to be on stilts.

This standard approach would not work for the scale of what we were creating. To solve this, we designed a series of supports, with concrete-grade beams capping the piles and vertical piers.

A pool area was created with a guesthouse attached, taking advantage of the lot's size as it creates a second setting for entertaining. In contrast to common practice for oceanfront homes, we placed the pool area on the bay side of the house, so as not to inhibit the views of the ocean from the main living areas. This also took advantage of the luxury of such a large property and kept the area under the house as free as possible.

Sure enough, when the Flop was completed, the clients threw a party to celebrate. Among the many guests invited were MRA's past clients. In fact, the friendships started that night are still active today.

"I think I'm just a frustrated architect."

A number of clients have said this to me in various forms, often at the initial meeting. My standard response is: "Really? So am I."

Architects have a particular relationship to creating houses. Houses traditionally have been laboratories for an architect's primary ideas about form, materials, and ethics.

On the one hand, there is the opportunity to realize something personal, whole, and expressive. On the other, sits the client. Yet if you free the house from the grip of commodity, it can say much about who we are and what we value. It can also, and more importantly, serve those housed, affecting their lives in very significant ways.

Houses designed by architects for particular sites and clients, are rare. A very small percentage of the population actually engages an architect to design and create a new home, making it crucial to accept the nature of the work. It is private and often hidden, and yet it has the power to challenge our accepted views; our expectations.

In most places, the participation of an architect is not a requirement to construct a house. Plans and documents must be submitted, but the requirements are gauged to ensure "health, safety and welfare." Housing, of which houses are a subset, has gone beyond the level of a commodity to become an economic index of sorts. Houses have become, and are expected to perform like, an investment. In a sense, they are burdened by this expectation, ultimately limiting their functional and expressive potential.

When someone engages an architect to create their house, they've let go a bit. They are faced with the potential of making a place that reflects their view of the surroundings, the environment, and their relationships with others.

STABLE AND BARN AT THE HANSON ESTATE
Constructed: 1918. Photo: 1993.

Those who do not study history are doomed to repeat it.

SHEAFF LANE

Sheaff Lane was not the first country house MRA built, but it is one of our most distinctive. From the very beginning, we were concerned with making a place that draws from the history of its surroundings. Because on Sheaff Lane, history had us surrounded.

The property sits down the road from a historic home called The Highlands. Built in 1796 by Anthony Morris, a Philadelphia merchant and politician, it was meant as a summer country residence – not to mention a safe haven to escape from the yellow fever epidemics literally plaguing Philadelphia at that time. It was also, coincidentally, the place where Randee and I were married in 1980.

Besides being populated by ghosts of past and present, the surroundings are genteel. With more of a country than suburban feel, it is the kind of place where people still keep horses.

In the early part of the 20th century, the original 300-acre parcel that had been owned by the Sheaff family during the 1800s was carved into pieces to build a number of Tudor estate homes.

History also provided us with an added burden. There was a restriction to the property's deed, stating that the new house must be in keeping with the buildings on the existing estate. While the restriction did not directly refer to a particular style, it was assumed that the language of the deed restriction was designed to ensure that a new Tudor Manse would rise on the property.

We had other ideas.

Taking a risk on a more stable environment

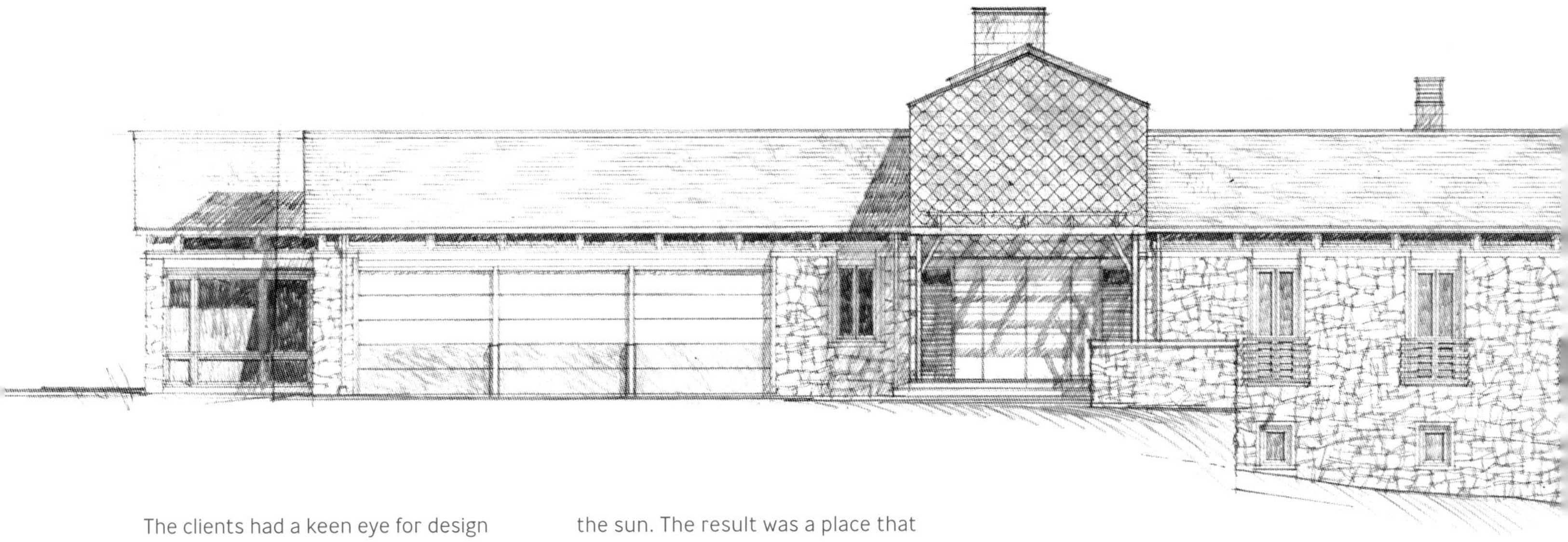

The clients had a keen eye for design and actively collected contemporary art. Now, with their children having left their primary home of 22 years, it was time to create a new setting for the next phase of their lives—one that would reflect their interests and celebrate their successes. While they wanted to take inspiration from the existing buildings on the estate, they weren't interested in living in a facile copy. And we weren't interested in designing one.

The existence of the deed restriction gave us access to the old estate and stable, so we could examine them for proper guidance. I quickly returned to the stable in order to spend more time there.

The stonework was particularly striking in its controlled rusticity and the openings were sparse. Masking the particular functions housed here, the building's form was simple, long, L-shaped, and primarily solid. In the rear, facing the pasture, large wooden doors created broad openings for the sun. The result was a place that appeared to predate the main house, despite its true history.

I left the property with the idea that our house should appear solid and functional, with simple forms of shelter. This impulse was confirmed later when I toured the area and encountered actual working stables. The clarity of the buildings and their arrangement struck me in a similar way. The construction revealed modest materials and detailing, but with a clarity of function.

I wanted something to appear as found and then re-inhabited. Something that predated the Tudor estate house.

Sheaff Lane would mark a new approach to creating houses for us—not through historical references, but rather through a reductive approach where the materials become the primary reference relating the house to the setting.

Three years after the completion of the house, the clients engaged us to refashion the area behind the house in a way that would promote the display of outdoor sculpture. We worked with Lisa Roth, a landscape architect who is credited on all six houses in this book. Lisa's work extends the intentions of our architecture and never attempts to conceal or soften the structures. The work on the sculpture garden began by redirecting the existing landscape, which sloped in a diagonal fashion behind the house, toward a stream.

By inserting a 270-foot-long retaining wall perpendicular to the house, the two-acre space would now relate directly to the house. Shifting the land at the wall eradicated the diagonal slope as it bisected the space into upper and lower "galleries." Plantings reinforced this and further defined areas, creating rooms for a growing collection.

At the end of the concrete wall, steel panels were erected to create an outdoor room behind them, bound by the woods located at the end of the garden. The client is a manufacturer and offered to fabricate the panels in his shop. Various finishes were discussed and we settled on used motor oil. It would act to preserve the metal on some level. Like diluted paraffin on a canvas jacket, the oil could be reapplied in the future, as the steel began to look dry. The steel walls immediately took on the attitude of unpredictability associated with age.

All rooms are created equal

While the clients had very specific ideas on room relativity—how the spaces should relate to each other—their view on style was as free as their restrictions were not. Their only desire was that the house should look quiet and unassuming, not formal.

My idea was to combine the various functions within building forms of equal size, four walls, and a roof, believing that the repetition of forms would fragment the large program into readable pieces. An early model revealed how the pieces could be assembled and where it could sit, on the edge of the meadow, looking towards the woods and stream.

After considerable editing, three major one-story buildings emerged: l. the main living/entertaining space; 2. garage/service/storage; 3. main bedroom/baths/office/exercise.

The three "barns" were equal in size—the sections were the same. Walls responded to the site orientation as well as function, but the rooflines were the same—simple sheltering gables of equal height, floating above walls separated by a continuous clerestory. The open ends were glazed in the same fashion, regardless of their location: living room, garage, main bedroom.

Knitting this together was a two-story piece containing the entry/kitchen/den with guest rooms on the second level, as well as a gallery separating the bedroom and service spaces.

The equal treatment in spite of function eroded the standard hierarchies present in traditional residences. The house would be picturesque because of its simplicity, not articulation and sculptural form.

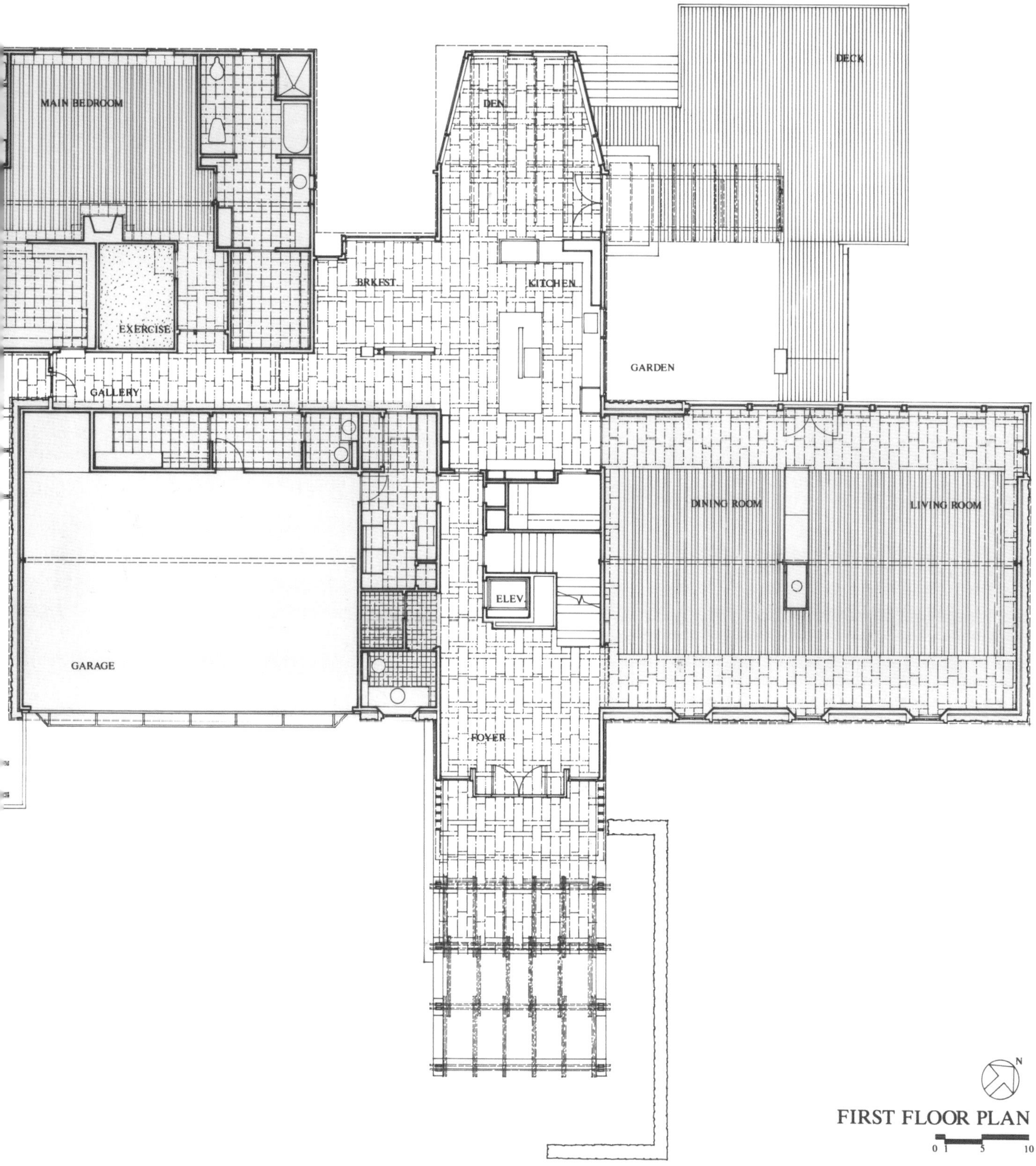

FIRST FLOOR PLAN

Once inside, the main living area is immediately apparent. The entire room can be read: the simple steel structure, braced in each direction; the clerestory separating the roof from the surrounding walls.

Both the walls and ceiling are made of plaster, left in its natural state and finished with a clear coat. There is a reflective quality to the surface. And at times the walls and ceiling take on the colors of the meadow.

Rebelling against the House of Tudor

At the conclusion of the initial design phase, we were required to submit plans and elevations for approval by the seller. I was confident that approval would be granted when consideration was given to the choice of traditional materials—stone, slate, weathered wood, and cedar.

I was wrong.

The design challenged too many formal expectations. It was not helpful that I had established rooflines with a slope more consistent with the requirements of the materials than the guidelines of traditional Tudor homes.

In order to settle the matter, an independent architectural consultant was engaged to arbitrate. Ultimately, we convinced the arbitrating architect—as well as the original owner—that our building would be humble and not diminish the integrity of the main house on the estate. Luckily for us, one such copy had recently been constructed along the road and the results served our side of the argument.

The clients had recently purchased a significant painting by Sean Scully. It would be hung in the foyer. They asked me to design a bench to sit in front of this. The idea was to create something that would appear to be made of light—something like ice. The bench was fabricated from polyester resin, twelve pieces stacked together in groups of four, with a hollow interior to capture the light from the foyer window.

A stair to the second floor guest rooms, wrapping around an elevator. The elevator would facilitate the moving of art from the basement storage area.

My clients could have caved to ensure that their house would be built, but they never did. They actually relished the idea that their house had challenged the restriction. They were eager to have their house take its inspiration from buildings meant to serve the historic land, not command it.

Timeless vs. Timeliness

There is something that reminds me of the temporal quality of a house. When visiting medieval castles surrounded by open fields, I am reminded that now long-gone houses once surrounded the castle in a dense array.

Their disappearance is not a cause for regret. The temporal quality, if accepted and realized, encourages me toward a freer expression that reflects the story behind the creation. Aside from technique, that is how things are made, accepting the eventual demise makes the past blurry and the future short. It focuses my efforts on the actual.

During my graduate studies at The University of Pennsylvania, Gabor Peterdi, a philosophical confidant of Louis Kahn, would roam the halls very late at night, giving unsolicited deskside critiques. He was not a professor at the time. The comments were always short and deep. The one I particularly remember is: "Architecture is what's left after the building burns to the ground." I get it. But for me this is the dark side of the "temporal." My reaction now would be: "Well then, we might as well make joy with everything above the foundation." Levity implies less gravity, and it's gravity that constricts the creation of a house.

I once viewed "timeless" as a positive attribute. It's a seductive term that implies a number of things, not the least of which is a small dose of immortality. It also infers the possession of deeper values as well as a connection to nature. My concern now is that "timeless" may actually be limiting, and the designation may transform into a clichéd style. A house designed is, at its best, an expression of its time. The materials, forms, systems, craftsmanship, spatial arrangement—everything points to the moment of its creation. So, my new goal is "timeliness."

Home Entertainment System

BAYVIEW

Getting away from it all and getting the party started may, at first glance, appear to be contradictory activities. However, that was the challenge our client offered us: To create a summer house that can serve as both a family retreat and an entertainment venue, all in an open and casual living atmosphere that flows around the bayside perimeter.

So ask yourself: What does a house become when it takes on a different character? How do you make a place where people feel comfortable – like they're not imposing upon a personal environment? How do you create that neutrality, yet provide spaces for the family to claim as their own?

Having always opted for more temporal materials that would weather, I felt that the stone should be used to define space, but not enclose it.

The walls could reach out to form a clear and quiet entry, welcoming guests while concealing outdoor spaces behind.

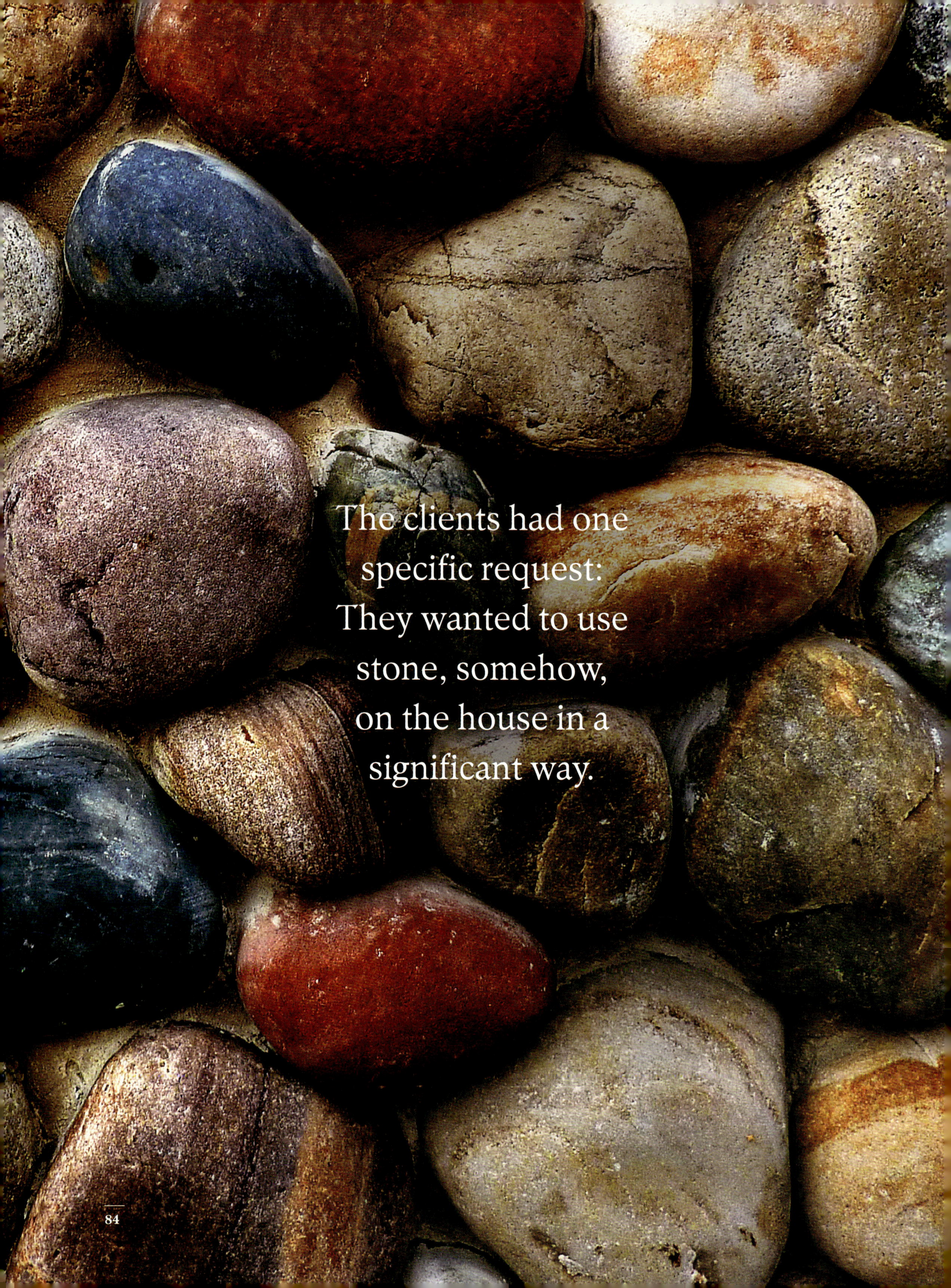

The clients had one specific request: They wanted to use stone, somehow, on the house in a significant way.

The use of stone ran counter to how I viewed houses at the beach. I was used to light materials; materials that weathered and were more temporal. The question remained: what type of stone to use here? A barrier island is made of sand, not stone. Stone is foreign to this environment. This reality eliminated the impulse to use stone that is local to the site. Viewing this as an opportunity to select something with other meanings, perhaps more personal, I thought of stones that were formed by water; literally shaped by water.

My earliest memories of water and swimming are of family trips to Central Pennsylvania in the summer. We would swim in the local streams: the water was crystal clear and I remember opening my eyes underwater, seeing an array of colored stones: browns, reds, tans, black. The walls could have a similar sense of discovery, as if the stone walls were here, with the house built around them.

Ultimately, Bayview was about recognizing the true nature, both socially and environmentally, of how a building will be used.

We quickly determined that the living spaces should flow around the bayside perimeter. As the 270 degrees of sweeping views take center stage, the shared living space creates neutrality where guests feel welcome as they come and go in a spontaneous, free-flowing manner, all while the family can claim a space for themselves.

In fact, each detail in the living areas aims to cultivate this casual, congenial atmosphere. From the large, communal dining room table that encourages a rotating cast of characters, to the sloped bridge that overlooks the living space and connects the wings for family and friends, movement is meant to be free and easy. Just like summertime.

Nearly 40 windows form the eastern wall, providing spectacular views of Barnegat Bay and marrying the house to its location.

Bayview provided us with another unique opportunity. The property was situated with 270 degrees of view, south to east, of the Barnegat Bay. The property has an odd shape, tapering from narrow at the road to the broad outside corner facing the bay. Water views to the north would be the most calm and serene with the sun striking the water from behind. This view would always have the greatest depth and color. The southwest view would be bright and reflective in the afternoons, the water turning silver in the reliable late-day thermal breezes.

WHAT'S THE HOUSE'S DEFINING CHARACTERISTIC?

The Great Wall of Windows. It's the best T.V. I own.

WHAT ARE VISITORS MOST SURPRISED BY?

That it's time to go home already

WHAT IS YOUR FAVORITE PART OF THE HOUSE'S INTERIOR?

Sunken family room. It's like a natural kid corral that they go into willingly!

WHAT WERE YOU MOST RELUCTANT TO LET MIKE DO?

Slope the bridge. I thought it should be level, but didn't have a reason why.

WHAT PART OF THE HOUSE HAVE YOU CHANGED YOUR MIND ABOUT?

The bridge.

An informal Q&A with the client offers a glimpse into the "living" part of what MRA likes to call a complete living environment.

WHY DID YOU BUILD THIS HOUSE?

Why not?

WHAT'S THE MAIN THING ABOUT THE HOUSE YOU HEAR FROM VISITORS?

The variety of interesting materials used. And when they're coming back.

WHAT'S YOUR FAVORITE ROOM?

Screen porch. You're not inside. You're not outside. You're just right.

WHAT DO THE CHILDREN SAY ABOUT THE HOUSE?

"It's better than the last hotel we stayed at." Did we mention we love kids?

WHERE IS YOUR FAVORITE PLACE?

Outdoor shower off the master bedroom. I never knew being naked outside could be so peaceful.

A single slab of dense bubinga wood forms this 11-foot-long table top. Versatile enough to seat 16 for a formal dinner without feeling "formal," it also accommodates buffet-style foraging—essential for when, say, 40 guests arrive for Memorial Day weekend.

The client was initially hesitant about the idea of a slightly sloped bridge (approximately eight degrees) between the two wings of the house. Now, it's regarded as one of the house's unexpected pleasures.

We often talk about glass as something that is simply transparent. However, the bridge reminds us of glass' reflective powers, revealing an entirely different view of the window wall, deck, and bay.

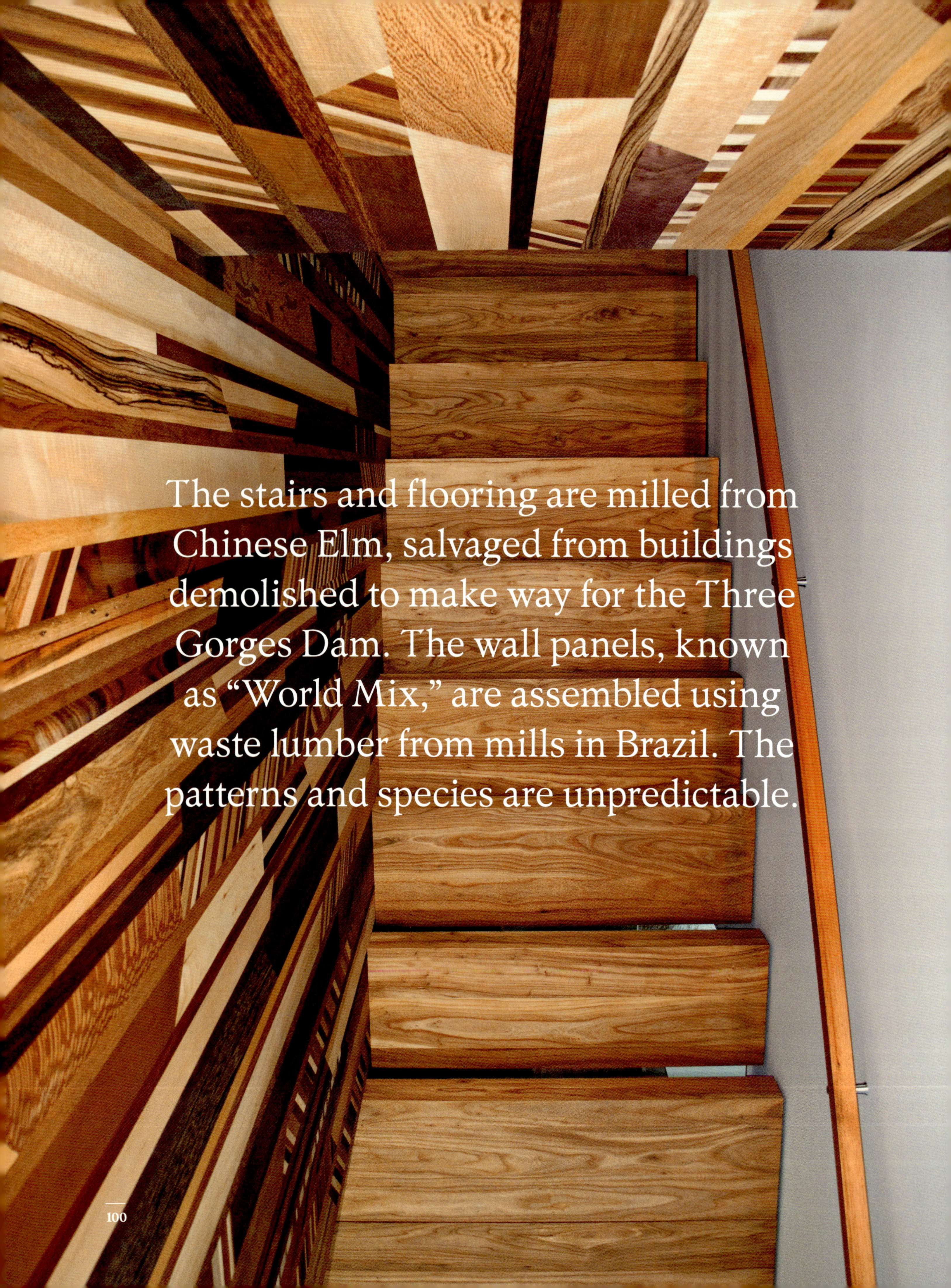

The stairs and flooring are milled from Chinese Elm, salvaged from buildings demolished to make way for the Three Gorges Dam. The wall panels, known as "World Mix," are assembled using waste lumber from mills in Brazil. The patterns and species are unpredictable.

With the prominence of the house's windows, much of the furnishing's colors and textures were created to match the color of the bay. In essence, we've brought the outside in, blurring the division of the two and forcing people to stop thinking in such terms.

In the end, there clearly was common ground between being homebodies and being hospitable. Currently, the clients are adjusting to life as young parents, and what was formerly used as a DJ booth is now optimized more as a place for stashing toys. Nevertheless, scores of guests continue to arrive during the summer months—along with UPS deliveries full of food and other sundries—so young and old alike can enjoy themselves. Bayview remains a place of celebration, in whatever form it may take.

Many clients th
working

nk twice about
with us.

BARN

It is a very small portion of the population that engages the long process of building a home with an architect. Rarer still are those who do this more than once in their lifetime. They, the repeat offenders, represent a particular personality type that enjoys the process as much as the material results.

MRA has been blessed with a large number of clients that fall into this category. It helps that the second time around is boosted by more familiar communication, not to mention an open trust of our convictions.

Fewer still are those who completely rebuild their home within the same structure twice. But that's what happened after Randee and I were invited to dinner with clients and now friends.

Two years after the completion of their beach house, the Flop, our clients would initiate the process of a complete reconfiguration of their primary home. For almost 20 years, they lived in what had been a Bank Barn, just outside of Philadelphia. Our discussions regarding a complete renovation had begun innocently enough.

The house had served our clients well over the years when they were raising their children. However, as their children had left home and their social lives had changed, it became clear that the house needed to change as well.

The rooms were adequate and well defined, but it was obvious that they were too confined. The living spaces were disconnected from each other as in a more traditional house. Another visible fact was that their art collections had grown beyond the ability of the space to display them. Additionally, they were now working from home and required a more substantial dedicated office area.

Dinner began with
a discussion about
additional lighting.
It ended with
a complete
renovation.

Finally, as they participated actively in various charitable organizations and had an ever-increasing number of friends, our clients had acquired an interest in food and entertaining. In fact, their parties were now centered on the preparation as much as they were on the serving. Dinner was now an open affair with no set menu—just good ingredients and an invitation to pitch in and get creative. At the Barn, the closed, hidden kitchen restricted this style.

Moving to a new home would have been the path of least resistance to the problems. But they didn't want to do that.

Finishing our meal, we brainstormed over the possibilities. It became clear that if we could expand the interior space by capturing the exposed outdoor roofed area, we could solve a number of problems. A new entry and stair on the ground level could free up space for a larger office. On the second floor this new space created by the porch's capture would become a gracious setting for the guests' arrival. And a large, flexible dining room would work here. In fact, it could all work.

The barn before the addition and renovation. A large covered area, exposed by the first renovation, would become recaptured and preserved within the house.

I viewed the old barn frame as an artifact now, not unlike the art collection my clients possessed. It was crucial that the frcme should be presented as such, as if it was in a gallery.

As I saw it, it was important to maintain the existing wood frame—a causal array of beams, posts, and braces. Unfortunately, the weathering over the preceding 20 years meant that the frame could not be considered a reliable structure.

Our solution was to float a steel frame at the elevation of the upper floor above the chestnut floor beams. The steel sections were made heavy, to be sized as thin and unobtrusive as possible. The depth, at eight inches, was more in scale with the wood. Steel columns with new foundations were set behind the original conical stone piers that supported the old wooden timber frame.

The new space, recaptured in a footprint 12-feet wide by 56-feet long, would free the existing interior spaces to be reconfigured in a way that would work for the next phase of our clients' lives. In essence, the reconfigured second floor would be designed as a single-level home. The kitchen could now be much larger and open, both horizontally and vertically, revealing the entire height of the original stone wall now exposed.

Three bedrooms on the third floor would still accommodate family and guests for occasional stays. Vast technical changes were made, improving the comfort of the large, open spaces.

The kitchen was expanded horizontally and vertically. We removed an underused den on the second floor to reveal the entire height and profile of the original stonework, which was entirely re-pointed.

In essence, the Barn was entirely rebuilt from the inside while it was being expanded. Ultimately, we were given the license to do what was right for the project and the building. Much of what you face as an architect has to do with dictating what you know—things that are measured, weighed, and counted. Things that are, in effect, objective. When an architect is faced with a structure like the Barn, the process is really one of discovery and continuous strategy to work within the given limitations and create something new.

Some of the best partnerships are built by hand.

A selection of projects constructed with builder Brian Smith

The relationship between architects and builders is as varied as the shades between black and white, constantly changing with time. Architecture, as a profession, was born of the role of the Master Builder. However, it is possible to view the development of the profession over time as a process of distancing the architect from the builder and associated trades.

From the outset, it became clear that my relationship with the fabricators of my work would be crucial to the success of the architecture. In fact, my ability to communicate intentions, priorities, and ideas would develop not only through how the work is physically documented, but also by understanding how long-term relationships could lead to a shared language.

The log frame immediately after the initial assembly. Window openings would be cut later.

Loglodge

I first met Brian Smith in 1994 while completing the design of a log home. I had worked with the clients previously on the renovation of a small beach house. This project would become their primary residence. After helping the client select a large parcel of land, they informed me that they would like to construct a genuine log home. I set aside my preconceived formal ideas for the house and embraced the material with the goal of understanding the technology, as well as the dimensional system dictated by log diameters and shippable lengths.

Brian was selected from a number of builders, not only because of his references but also by virtue of his personality. We had the sense that he was not daunted by the complexity of the system. The most crucial task of the entire project was the erection of the pre-cut log structure that would arrive to the site one truck at a time. The entire truckload had to be erected within a long workday, or penalties could be levied. Seven days—and truckloads full of logs—after the process began, they were fully assembled.

Frenchtown

Every project is required to work through the issue of value, but especially so on a limited budget. The project involved modernizing a 1930s bungalow and adding a significant extension. The question was: How to make this generic structure a part of a dwelling that could accommodate contemporary life?

The old bungalow would become the domestic side: bedrooms, baths, library, and kitchen. The new portion would be the spaces to accommodate the studio, entry, dining, and entertainment. Re-making older domestic structures is like taxidermy. Brian worked to stabilize the bungalow and refit the spaces with new systems. Concrete floors were sealed and metal frames were employed to support new, double-story walls. Ultimately, we were able to preserve a historic structure while also making it new.

This project with Brian involved re-purposing a 1930s bungalow along with an extension encompassing the more public spaces of the house.

THE UNPUBLISHED COLE PORTER
great songs of broadway

I find that the work becomes less clinical when the maker becomes collaborator. We are more likely to experiment with new systems and techniques, making the process open to discovery.

Rocky Hill

Three years later, Brian was selected from a number of bidders to build a home near Princeton, New Jersey. In general, fear drives the bidding process, in part due to the unknowns of working with new people: architects and clients. Our previous work on Loglodge eliminated this factor. With a shared history in place, the work becomes less defensive and the capacity for fabrication informs the design. Many of the same craftsmen were employed to achieve a different end.

The clients had selected an extremely rocky site with tall trees that mute the daylight. The house is designed to sprawl, with all spaces on a single floor. Roof lines reach up to capture the sky above the trees. The goal was to create a light-filled environment, varied through plan and volume.

Under the best of circumstances, creating a meaningful house is the result of being in this moment of creation, without the irrelevant distractions of taste and personal identity. My work is often focused on removing and eliminating, as much as designing, viewing the process like clearing a path.

The path metaphor supports my belief in what I call the best "inevitable house," which sits at the end of the path. It's as if such a house exists for every opportunity to create one and my goal is to both shape and reveal it.

The "inevitable house" has a primary condition: it must be achievable. It's quite different from the "ideal house," often the architect's impulse, or vision, functioning as a starting point in the process. When a house is finished, I often look back through the documentation to understand the path of creation.

Doing this reveals a general paring down, editing, and often abandonment of initial impulses with entire schemes, eventually flipped in mirrored fashion.

The houses then seem to congeal through fabrication, previous techniques informing the current, leading to the next. My philosophy tends toward consequence more than ideals.

I THINK I MA

I want to build another house.

BIG INDIAN

Those were the first words I heard over the phone from a past client. The house I had built with him years earlier, on the bayfront of Long Beach Island, had been a large and—at times—stressful endeavor. Luckily for me it had turned out very well, and he was still enjoying time there with family and friends.

This new house would also be a shared space designed to accommodate rotating groups of guests; one where the key would be left under the front doormat. Nestled up in the Catskills, it would be a base for fall and winter activities as well as family gatherings. If you could find it, and there was an empty room, you would be welcome to stay.

The idea was to create a building that was, like a rock itself, all stone and concrete. Slate tiles on the walls and roof, with gravel on the exposed roof areas of the lower level. Almost like a core sample taken from the ground, each layer affecting the degree of enclosure.

Sometimes
a house is
actually a
bridge.

20%

The builder's name was Wolfgang. A native of Dresden who escaped the Iron Curtain in 1958, he was all muscle and no B.S. As I was describing my full-service approach, there was an uncomfortable pause. Wolfgang asked, "So Michael will be approving all payments to the builder?" When the client answered yes, Wolfgang said without apology or hesitation, "Then that will be an additional twenty percent."

The client then suggested I ride with Wolfgang to the site at the top of the hill. He gave me a look that made it clear I would have to make the twenty percent disappear.

And I did.

Architecture requires an ability to work alongside others. Our work, at its simplest, defines others' work. I needed to erase a common view of architects as a hinderance. My conversation with Wolfgang turned toward topics that reinforced this. I saw that he was truly interested in buildings and sensed that he could relish a different approach. From that time forward, Wolfgang supported our vision and never caused conflicts with my intentions.

The lot was wooded but not lush, due to the rocky soils. The under story was relatively clear, making our navigation a bit easier. I mentioned that we should obtain a survey that would indicate the topography. Wolfgang shrugged this off as unnecessary. We discussed our options and began to measure slopes at a few key areas. On the way down, he asked if I would like to see his house; a gesture of trust. Later, I learned that this was a rare occurrence.

Viewfinder

As I stood on the downhill slope of the site, through the recently leafless trees, I could see Belaire Ski Mountain in the distance as it broke the horizon defined by the ridge to the west.

At that moment, I felt that the house should be sited, not only to defer to this view, but also to frame it. A house in the woods creates a clearing and I pictured the clearing as a bowl, with the house down in it. The far edge of the bowl would be the ridge, with Belaire creating a third layer beyond.

From the approach road, the house fulfills its role, framing the distant landscape.

When you think you're there, turn right.

Early designs yielded a casual grouping of spaces. The client approved immediately. But something was still lacking for me. I reconsidered the realities of the winter, the fact that everything seems to cling to life here. The trees to the rocks and the people to the small towns. The building needed to be tougher.

So I took the top level and I rotated it to form a cross over the lower level. The house, now cantilevered and clinging to the rock ledge on the side of the mountain, framed the distant landscape and fulfilled its role as a resilient, rugged structure.

The main room is in a long-building form that shelters the entry, service spaces, porte-cochere, and garage—all under one roof supported by a log structure.

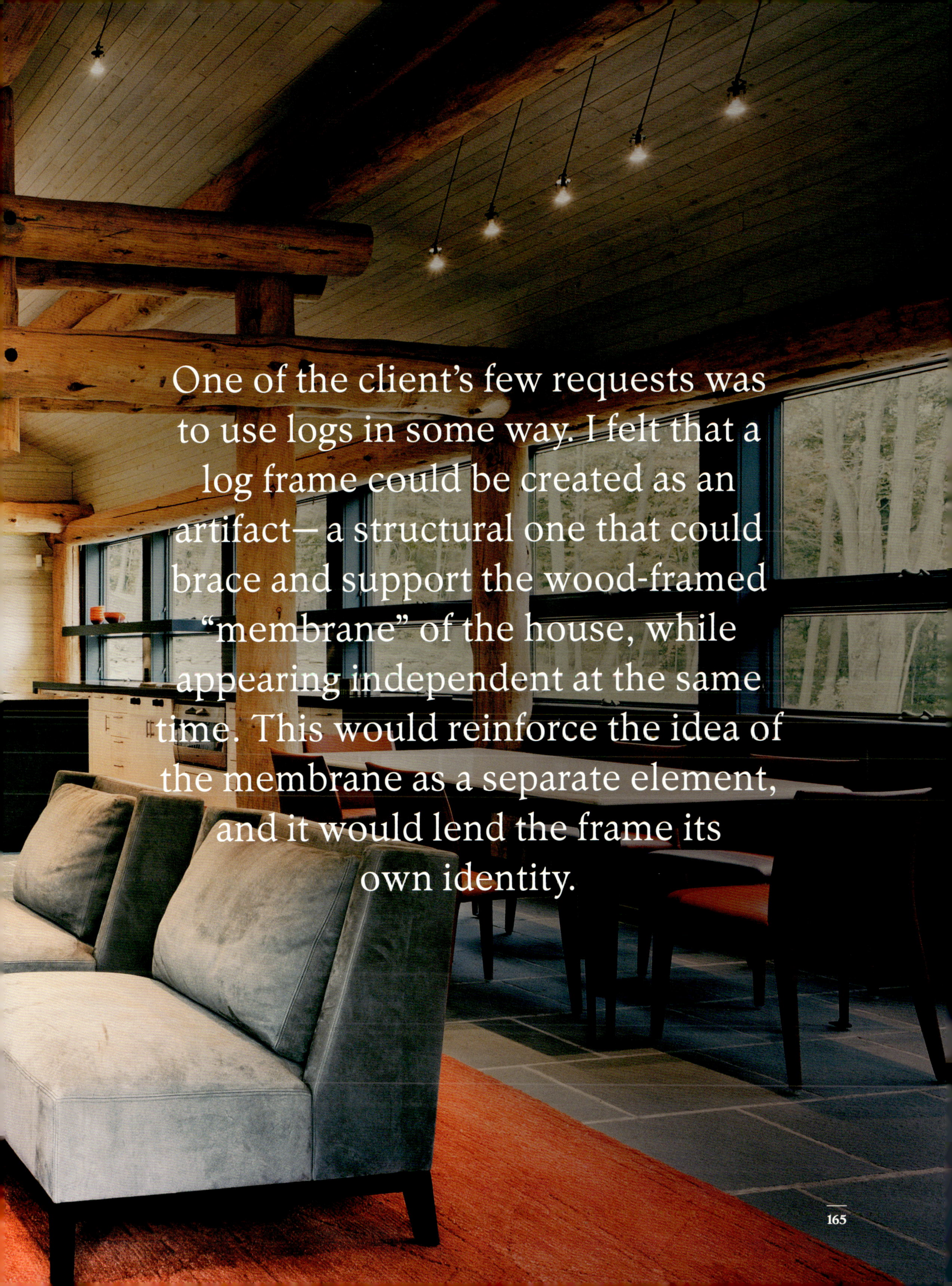

One of the client's few requests was to use logs in some way. I felt that a log frame could be created as an artifact—a structural one that could brace and support the wood-framed "membrane" of the house, while appearing independent at the same time. This would reinforce the idea of the membrane as a separate element, and it would lend the frame its own identity.

The interior surface is white cedar, which adds a luminous, soft quality and serves as a neutral background. It also replaced the standard use of drywall or plaster.

The large scale of the window at the end of the house contrasts with the small seating area, giving the room the vertiginous effect of being situated right over a precipice.

Yet, it is highly comfortable, especially sitting adjacent to the fireplace and overlooking the mountain ridge and winter snowfalls.

“So, what are your top 10 bands?”

This is a crucial question asked of all potential new hires at the firm.

Winchester Cathedral

Bem Vinda Vontade

Transparent Things

Everything's Perfect

Blood Money

Auspicious Winds

Doubt

Over-nite Sensation

Garvey's Ghost

Hot Rats

Biograph

My continued interest in contemporary music is indirectly influential as it represents a continuous search for something new; something that makes everything previous sound a bit boring.

In many ways, this is similar to our clients' expectations with regard to their environments. Being open to the new in both art and music is an ethical imperative for me. This curiosity is a significant part of the culture at MRA. It serves to keep our visions broad and the critiques of our own work continuous.

A Ghost is Born
Safe as Milk
Black Stars
A Series of Sneaks
Let Go
The Doldrums
Brighten The Corners
Rather Ripped
Castaways and Cutouts
Only Life
Four Winds
The Outsider
Team Boo

TIME A

ND TIDE

Time is an inescapable element in the creation of a house. Certain conditions inevitably dictate the duration of a project. Seasonal aspects enter when the house is seasonal itself, demanding completion for the summer season. The lives of the clients are also crucial to time. For Ocean Retreat, it was both of these factors. And then some.

The clients wanted a house that would be openly shared by their extended family. Children were still at an age that ensured participation. Cousins appeared to be best friends. But this time would not last. And the sudden development of a health issue with the client made time all the more critical.

They had purchased an oceanfront property where the existing house was insignificant —a copy of the suburban model of the time, except raised on woodpiles. The land, however, was quite significant with its long exposure directly overlooking the beach. Other lookers had passed on the opportunity, viewing the "guarded" (read lifeguards) beach as a disturbance to an imagined solitude. Guarded beaches are few in the town of Loveladies, and this one served the bayside community of Loveladies Harbor as well. The clients actually cherished this aspect of the site. They viewed the activity as positive, enjoyable, and also, practical.

As part of the purchase, they would not take possession of the property until August 15th. The hope was to have it completed for the following summer. In total, we had 18 months to design and build the home.

Others had passed on the property, viewing the guarded beach as a disturbance to an imagined solitude. The clients actually cherished this aspect of the site. They viewed the activity as positive, enjoyable and also, practical.

Retreat does not mean surrender

Calling this house a retreat has two interpretations. Both are valid but have more meaning when combined. The first implies an escape from the everyday; the second speaks to a gathering of people. Rather than a place to simply escape as in a solitary way, gathering would be crucial and the house would have to promote this.

Banking on previous approaches, initial schemes explored separate houses within one, with the goal of creating privacy for various families. But I kept coming back to the "guarded" beach they so cherished and realized what they really desired: a single large, shared living floor; a place that would accommodate everyone, at various activities, but on one level. Bedrooms could be gathered together on the floor below.

The spaces are designed to reflect the clients' values: everyone together, up top, with the best views and the coolest breeze.

99d

A full house beats a pair

Placing the living areas on the uppermost floor offered dramatic views of the ocean and horizon while showcasing the active beach populated with umbrellas, chairs, toys, and the wind-scattered sounds of people having fun.

The architecture is detailed to step aside and simply frame the views. Variety is not stylistic but lies in the placement of openings relative to the various spaces. The windows are set wide but low in the living area to accommodate those seated with a beautiful ocean vista. The tall windows of the dining area capture the sky. Glass doors pocket away to allow screens to transform the screen porch into a portion of the deck.

From the beginning, the house was full. A growing problem was the pile of sneakers and sandals in the foyer. To solve it, we would design shelves to stack them and a wall piece with hooks for car keys. It's a true measure of success that these elements are the only decoration in this space. Upon arriving, you immediately can count the occupancy and see the variety of identities. Just add your sandals and you're in.

Years later, despite the changes in their lives, the house continues to be a gathering place for the family. It brings to mind that, like people, houses contain stories. They don't exist as static pieces on a disconnected landscape. It's possible that a house will reflect a private generosity that continues and outlives the creator. You can't tell by simply looking.

Let's end at the beginning.

There is a question about influence: What most influences one's work? Is it the time when you are educated, or the time when you are born? Nature, or nurture?

I don't know the definitive answers, but I can only speak to the influences that have defined me as a person and an architect. And the combined collection of my experiences continues to influence the decisions I make today.

I was raised in a two-story rowhouse in Chester, Pennsylvania, a city located on the Delaware River 15 miles south of Philadelphia. The river was used to transport goods from numerous oil refineries, chemical plants, and a large shipyard. Everyone seemed to work at one of these places—half of them inside; the others, outside. Before the days of environmental consciousness, the sky was eternally lit by the open flares of industry. It was never dark. Hazy summer nights glowed orange.

Our rowhouse was small (in current terms: 880 square feet = 20 x 22 x 2). It was built immediately after WWII as part of the effort to house returning soldiers. In 1994, my childhood home would inspire my entry into a national "Affordable Housing" competition. Suffice it to say, the resourcefulness of small spaces—the subtle yet significant ways in which they can be made inviting rather than confining—had an impact on me.

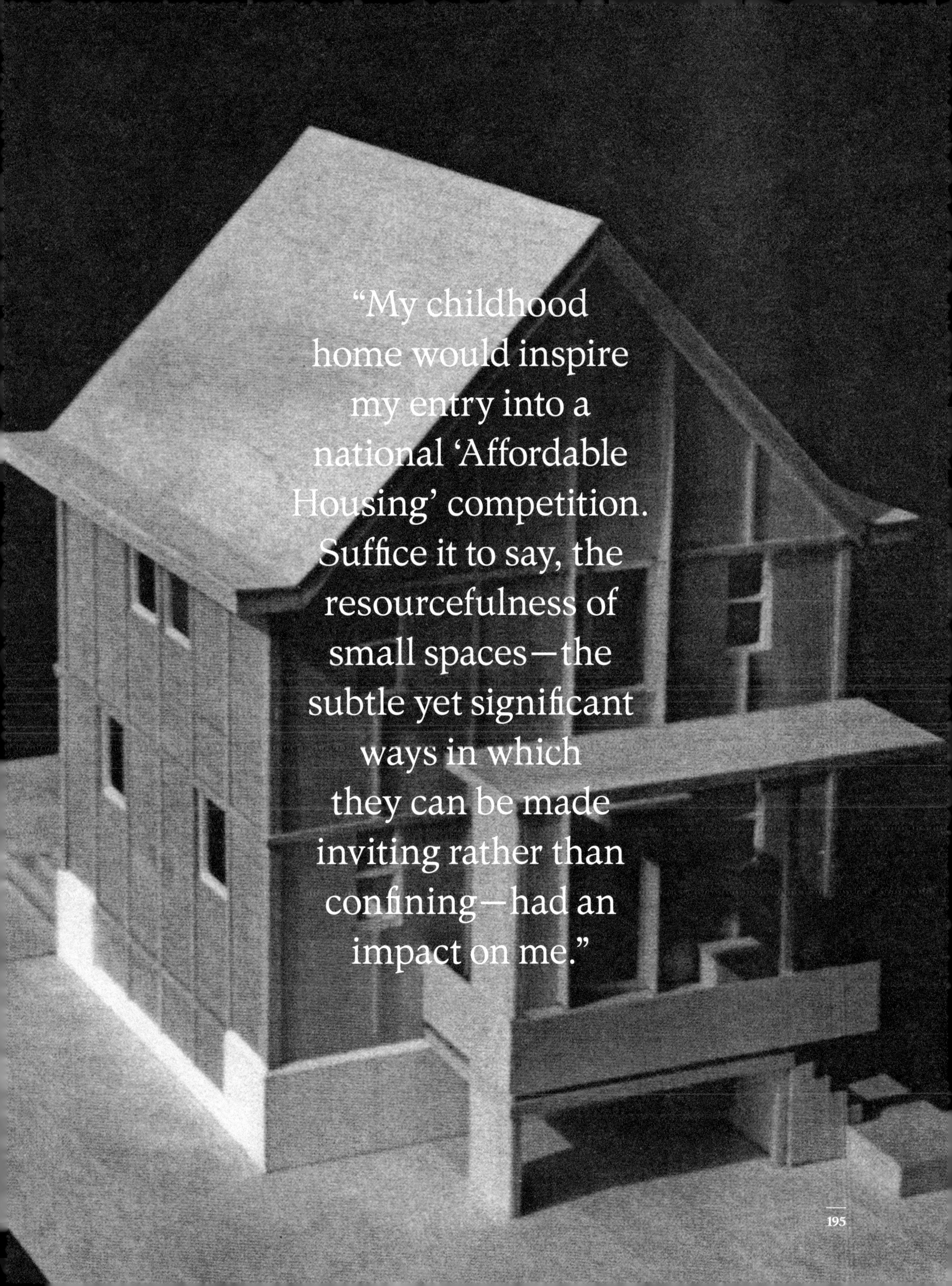

"My childhood home would inspire my entry into a national 'Affordable Housing' competition. Suffice it to say, the resourcefulness of small spaces—the subtle yet significant ways in which they can be made inviting rather than confining—had an impact on me."

One week of every childhood summer was spent in a cabin at World's End State Park. The relationship between the elemental materials of these simple structures and their surrounding location left a lasting impression on me.

I've been told that I have an obsession with stairs. I've tried to justify this in architectural phrasing like, "They are transient places, and are experienced by moving through them, unlike rooms." However, the obsession is actually linked to the stairs in my childhood house, which, ironically, were not really transient at all. People sat on the first two steps and the landing. It was where guests would perch. Memories of passed relatives are framed with its backdrop. The landing was a chair, with a stair attached.

My house is not the only building from my childhood that still resonates. As a toddler, my family's summer vacation was a week in a state-owned cabin. My parents would apply as early as possible to secure the weeklong rental, which cost $15. The cabins were located in a park called "World's End" and constructed as a WPA project in the 1930s. They were elemental, dark, and sheltering. It felt as if they were made from the forest floor. It was here where I first realized the connection between structure and the natural world just outside.

Alternately, we spent time on the New Jersey Shore, first in Wildwood and eventually in Avalon. We would rent an open room with a small kitchenette, two double beds, and a bath. As with the mountain vacation, most of our time was spent outside, in the water, on a porch, or visiting friends. These experiences further reinforced the idea that a structure often works to facilitate happy experiences and memories in the environment beyond its footprint.

"People sat on the first two steps and the landing. It was where guests would perch. Memories of passed relatives are framed with its backdrop. The landing was a chair, with a stair attached."

A streetscape in Bavaria, 1972

The Church of Santo Spirito in Florence, Italy, 1977

I decided that I would be an architect at age eight. When you consider my family history this may not seem so unusual.

My father spent his working years as a draftsman at an oil refinery. When he retired, his work had touched every portion of the expansive plant. In addition, my mother's father was a mason who emigrated from Naples. He and his brothers had built some of the major buildings in Chester: St. Anthony's Church and the Masonic Hall, among others.

What is perhaps unusual, however, is that my father's work and this family history never entered our house. While I may have correctly predicted my future vocation at age eight, this childhood impulse to become an architect did not grow from a direct consciousness of work as career or vocation. Nevertheless, building things is clearly a part of my lineage.

So back to the question of influence. It would ultimately take a liberal high school education to expose me to the broader world of art and consequently, architecture. My parents sacrificed the move to the suburbs in order to send my brother and me to Archmere Academy, in Delaware. Archmere's primary feature is a large Italianate mansion that was built between 1916-1918 by John J. Raskob, who would go on to build the Empire State Building. The house did not contain classrooms but served as housing for a small number of boarding students along with the teaching priests of the Norbertine Order. The building was of a type I had never experienced before. All I had known up to that point were small houses, churches, parochial schools, and factories. The mansion, thrown into sharp relief, showed me that buildings had the capacity for grandeur and possibility.

These lessons were further enhanced by my high school art teacher, Stephen Rossi, who taught me drawing, painting, printmaking, and history for three consecutive years. In addition, I convinced two teachers and three other students to travel throughout Bavaria, Northern Austria, and Switzerland in a van in the summer after my second year, when I was 15. Like many impressionable teenagers before and after, Europe truly broadened my senses.

When I arrived at Penn State in 1974, the World Trade Center was a year old, and Louis Kahn had died five months before. Robert Venturi's "Complexity and Contradiction" was the new thinking, but the halls still smelled of modernism and what became coined as brutalism. Yale's fire in Paul Rudolph's A&A building seemed to be a verdict on the decadent progression of modernism. The hippie architects turned social programming into a science, with an entire studio dedicated to the analysis of a single project. At the same time, utopian approaches by Archigram, Archizoom, Ant Farm, and the Jersey Devils were on our radar. Paolo Soleri lectured about Arcosanti, which, innocently enough, seemed entirely feasible at the time.

In 1977, the spring term of my junior year, I was in Italy preparing to study at the University of Florence. This was challenged, and ultimately enhanced, by the closing of the University due to a student strike led by the Communist Party. Instead of having us return home to Penn State, Dean Raniero Corbelletti instructed us to stay and draw. He told us that the city was now our classroom. The church of Santo Spirito was in a neighborhood relatively free of tourists. I was fascinated with the external simplicity and effect of weathering on the façade—another aspect that had a profound effect on me and continues to feature prominently in the spaces I design today.

My summers during college were spent working in construction: painting, carpentry, and masonry. I never sought to work in an office during this time. There was an immediate satisfaction drawn from transforming and creating something tangible. Despite the work being difficult and often misguided, I was exposed to the relationship between work and buildings; that architecture was, on a certain level, defining the work of others. Buildings were no longer finished and static. I began to view them as having had, at their inception, an active life of labor, economics, desire, and random determination.

"My solution for student housing was simply, houses—large, shared houses. Spatial variety was randomly imposed, rather than designed. I took a similar approach with an art center in the historic residential neighborhood of Society Hill in Philadelphia. The studios were metal barns; simple shelter."

At Penn State, I was uninterested in heroic buildings. Instead I was drawn to the everyday and the common. In my first design studio, under Julian Weiss, my solution for student housing was simply, houses—large, shared houses. Spatial variety was randomly imposed, rather than designed. I took a similar approach with an art center in the historic residential neighborhood of Society Hill in Philadelphia. The studios were metal barns; simple shelter.

Student Housing at Penn State, 1975

Print Club of Philadelphia, 1978

Master's thesis, modelled on a housing competition for ten "machiya," or traditional urban houses in Kyoto, 1980

"I knew I had to ignore others' expectations and simply follow my inspiration. I was determined to work on the projects that mattered to me."

Through Journals like *GA (Global Architecture)*, edited by the photographer Yukio Futagawa starting in 1970, I was exposed to the contemporary residential architecture of Japan. It was born of spatial necessity, a clear approach to materials and an open view of what constituted a residence.

The work stood in contrast to the hierarchical tenets of Post-Modernism. The work grew from a view of fabrication and craft. It was very personal and idiosyncratic. The fascination led me to model my master's thesis on a housing competition for ten "machiya," or traditional urban houses, in Kyoto. The site addressed various conditions: houses on the street with small shops and houses on an alley. I viewed this as a format to frame the study of traditional building crafts and to explore the intimate scale of city houses within a strictly defined context.

At the time, students were discouraged to pursue a thesis of this nature. Typically, thesis projects were institutional in nature: university buildings, museums and the like. Nevertheless, I knew I had to ignore other's expectations and simply follow my inspiration. I was determined to work on the projects that mattered to me.

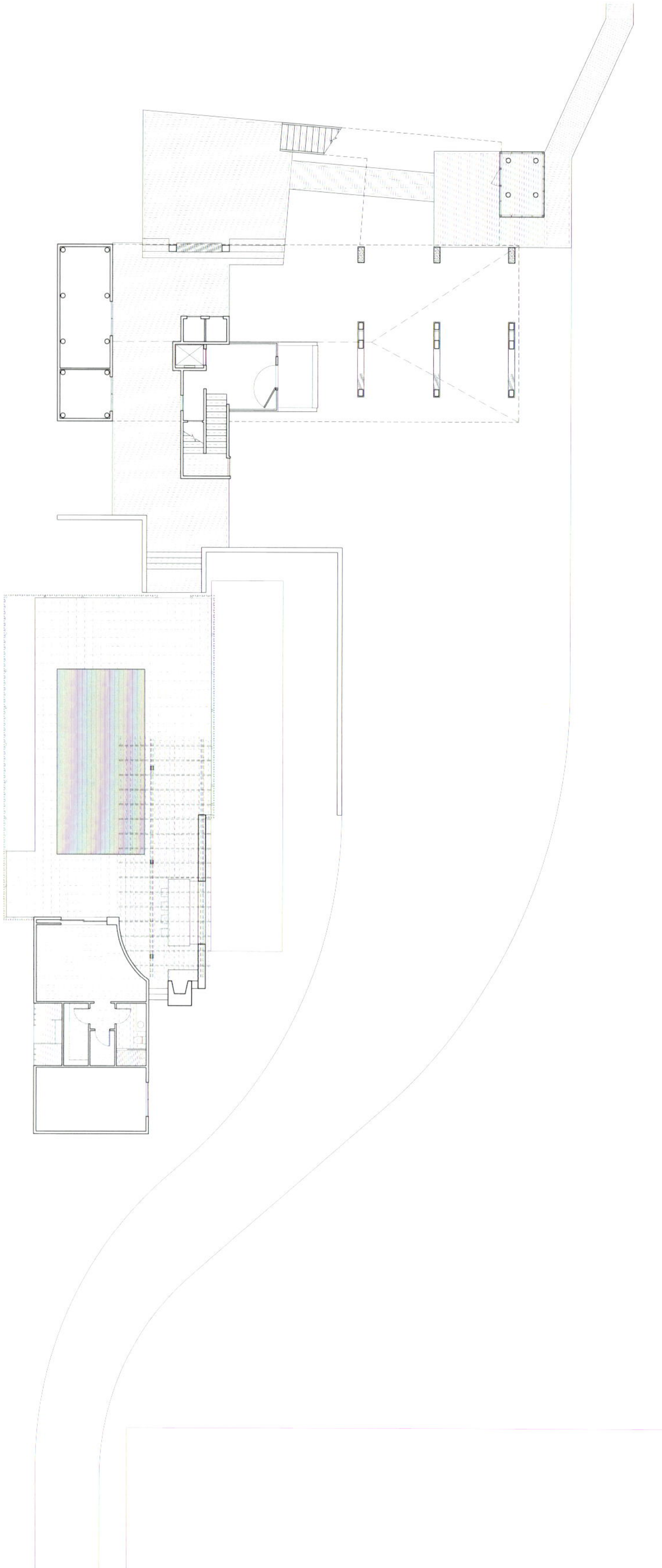

Site Plan

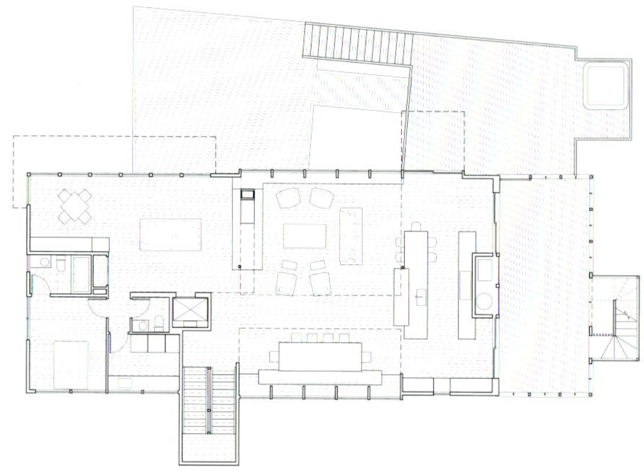

Living Floor Plan

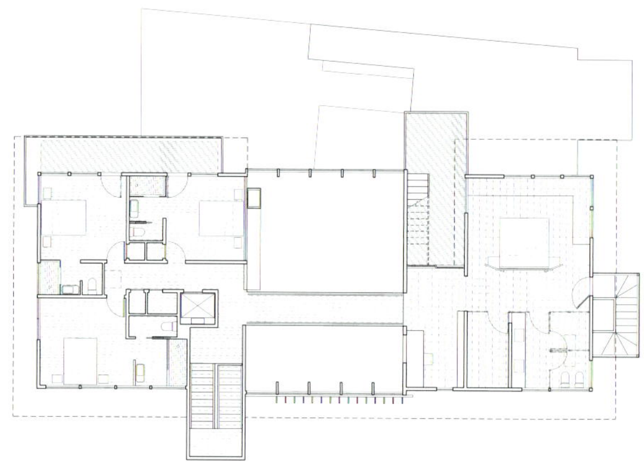

Bedroom Floor Plan

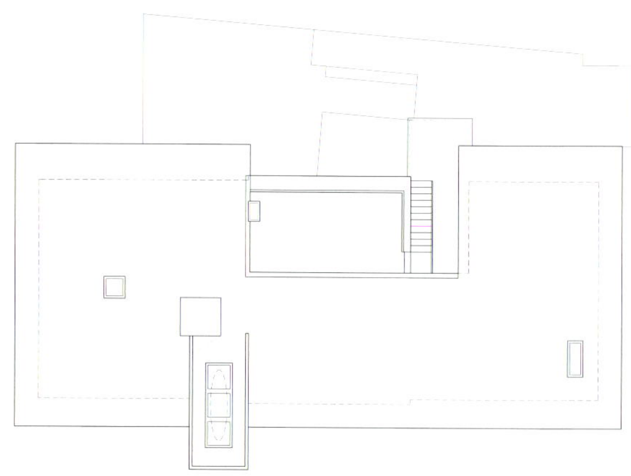

Roof Floor Plan

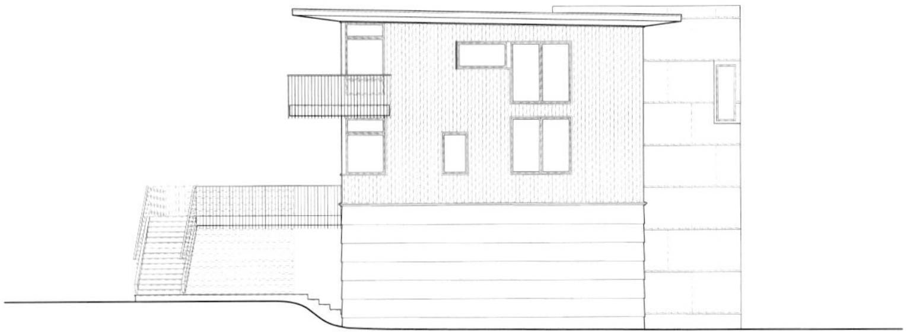

North Elevation

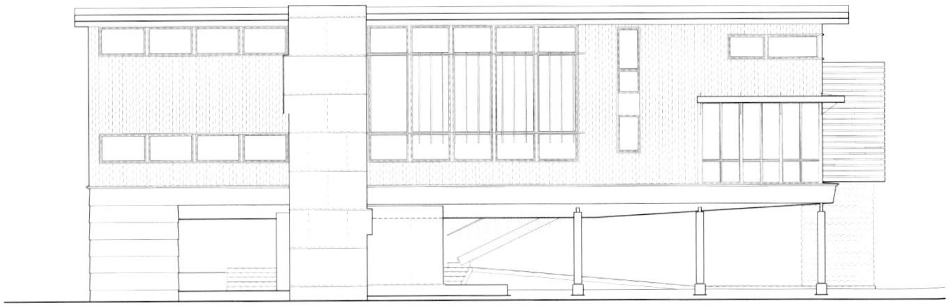

West Elevation

South Elevation

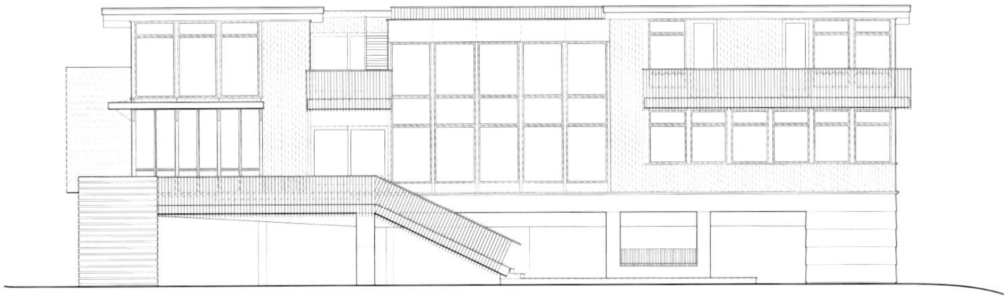

East Elevation

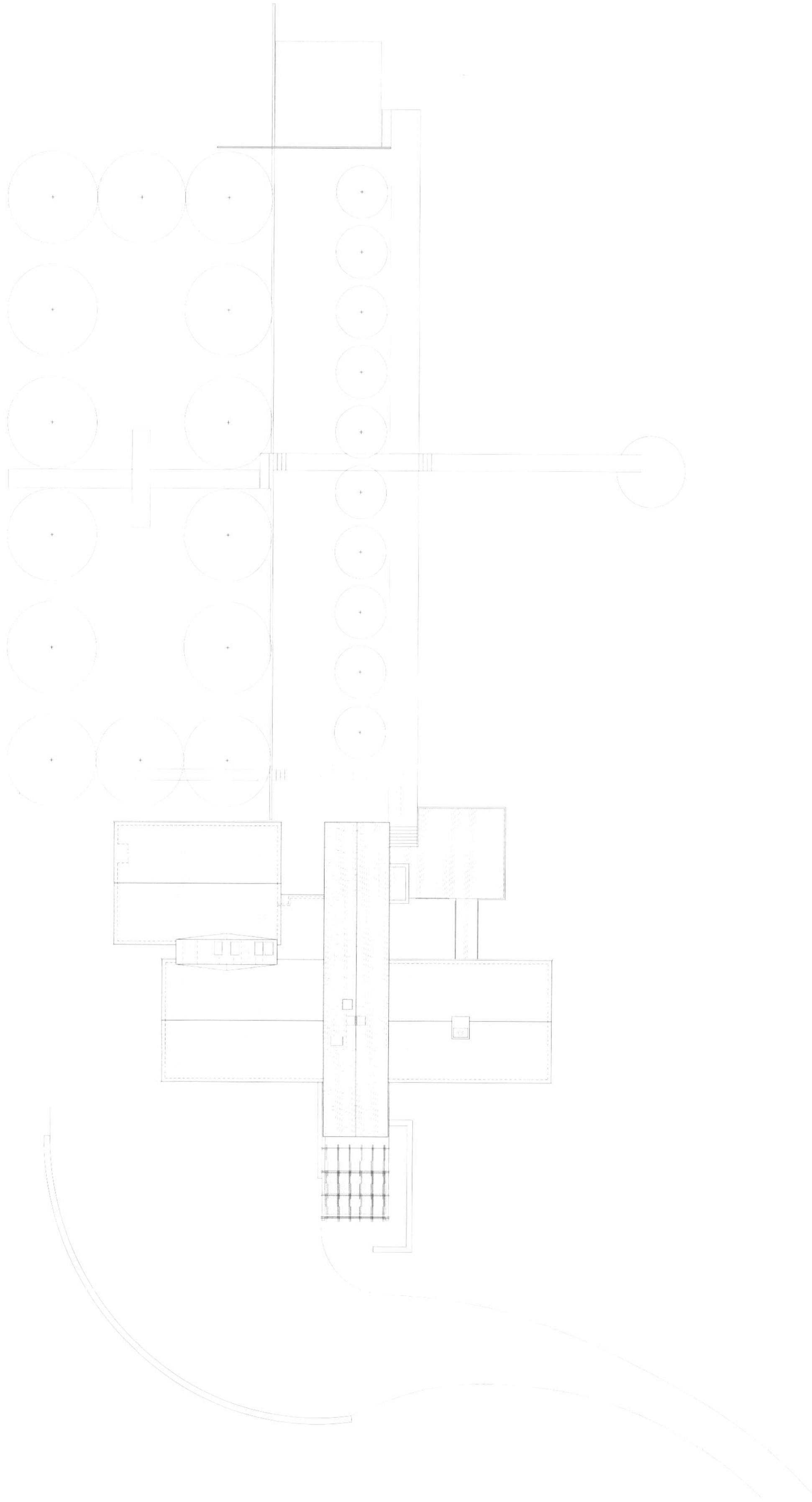

Site Plan

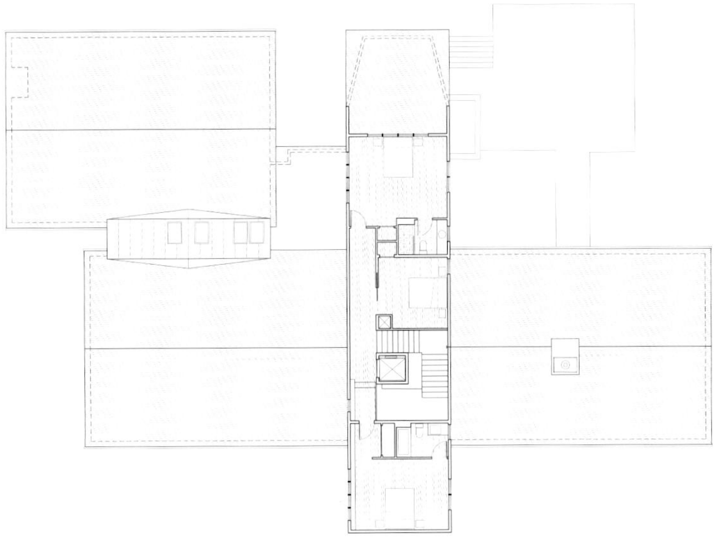

Second Floor Plan

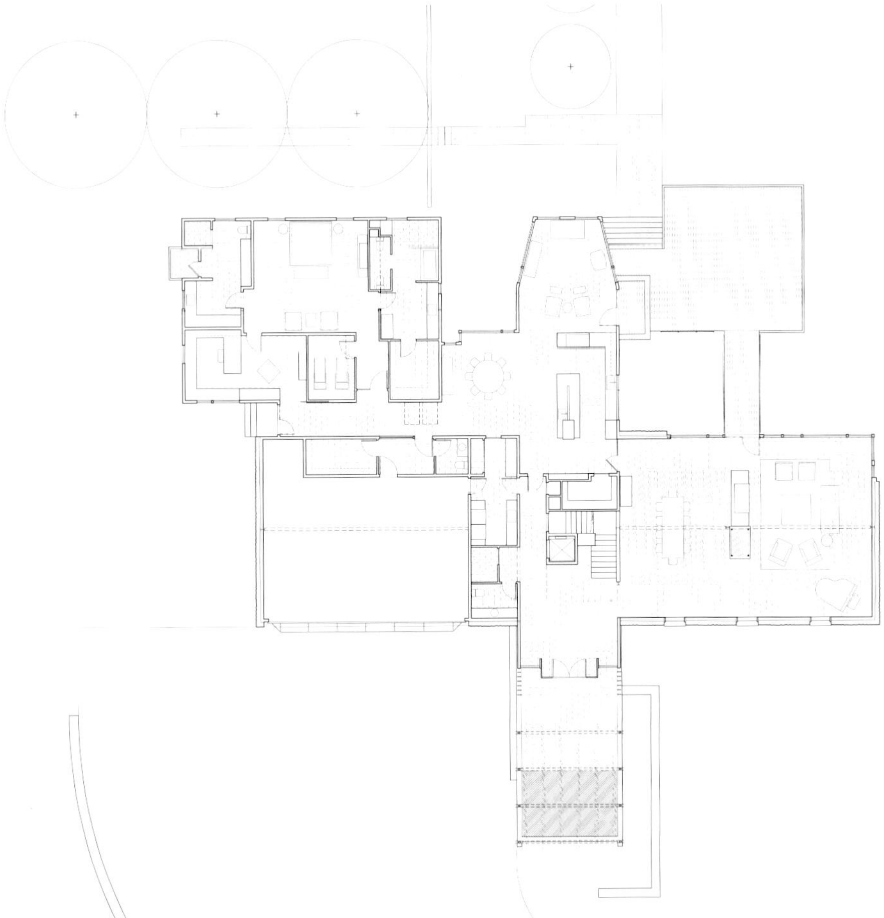

First Floor Plan

North Elevation

East Elevation

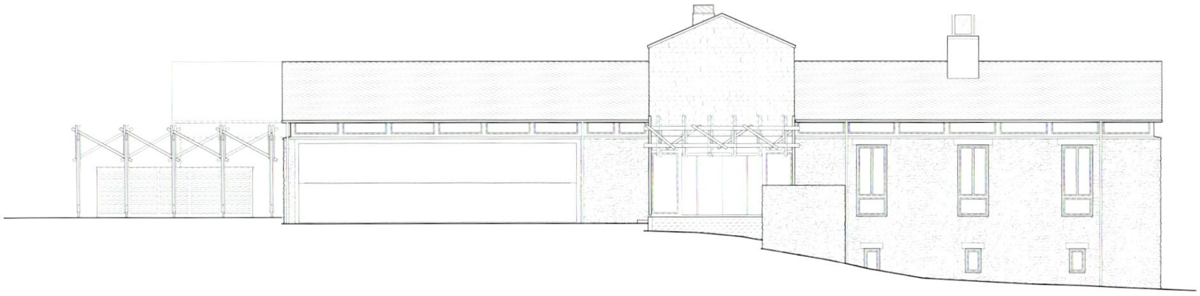

South Elevation

West Elevation

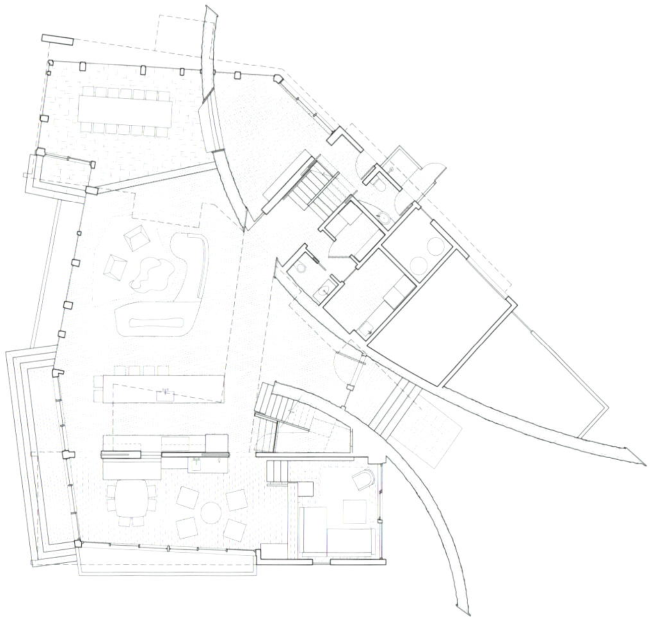

Living Floor Plan

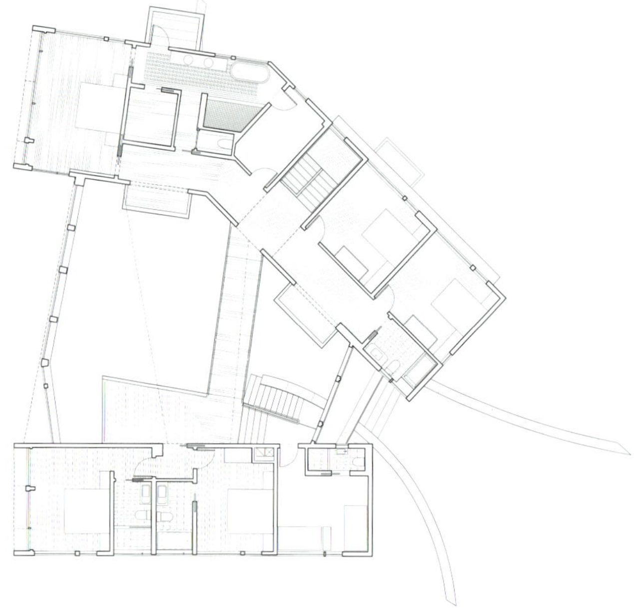

Bedroom Floor Plan

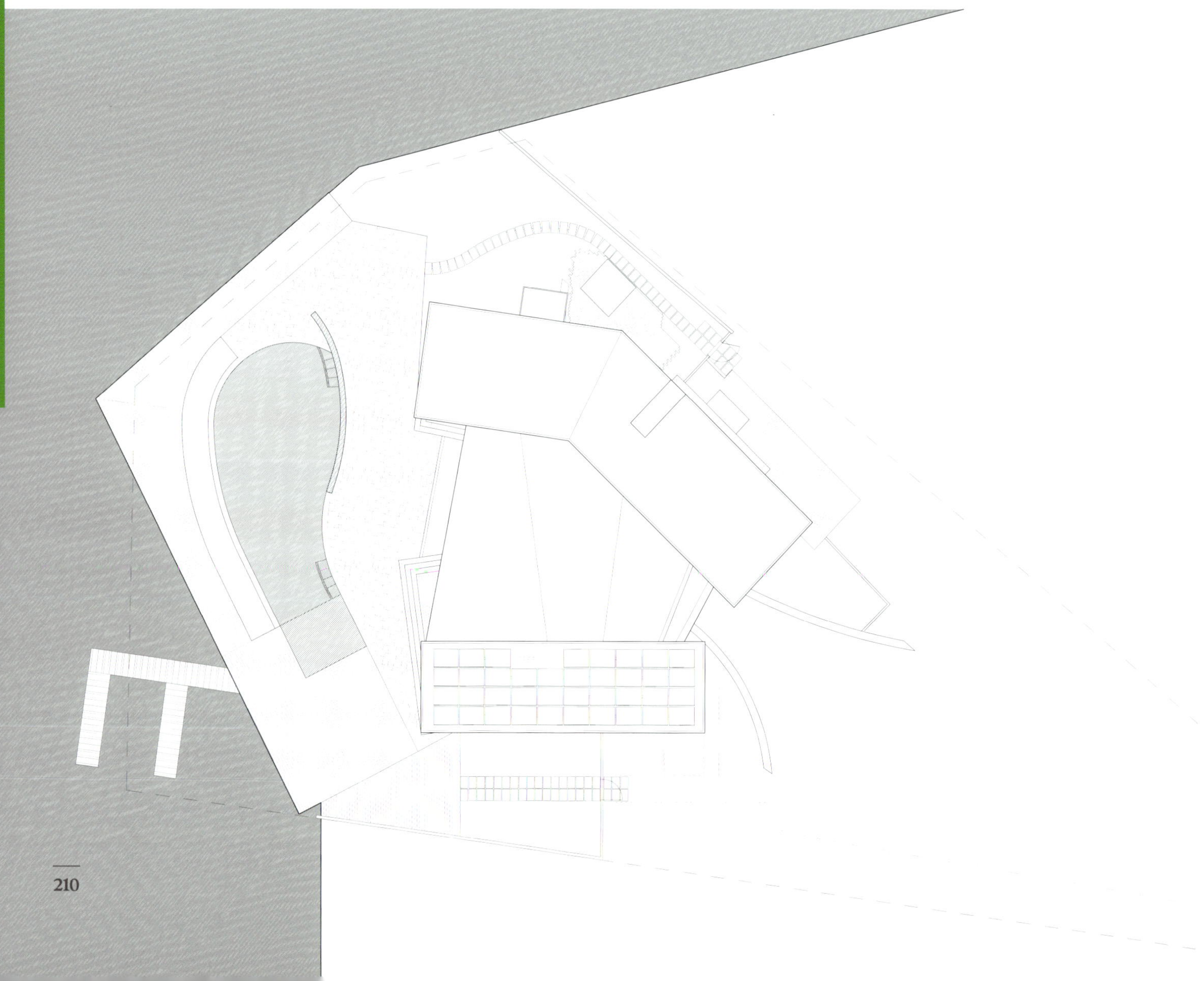

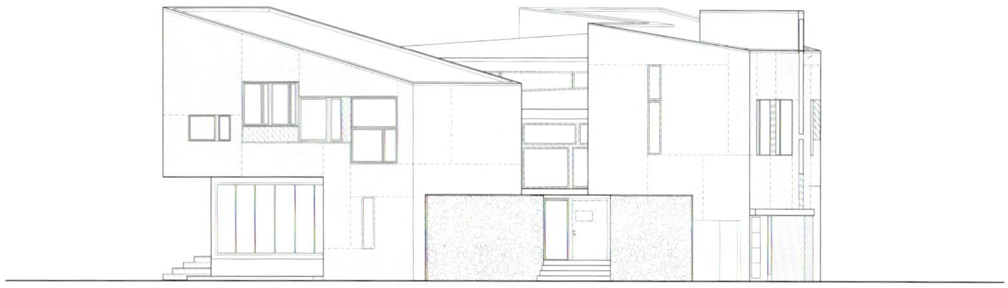

East Elevation

North Elevation

West Elevation

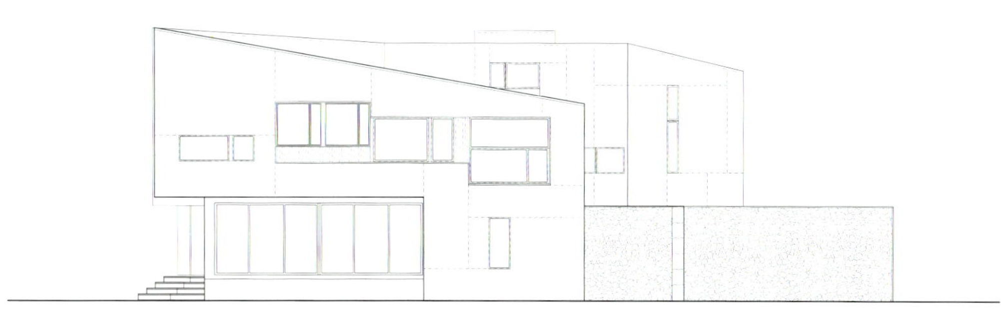

South Elevation

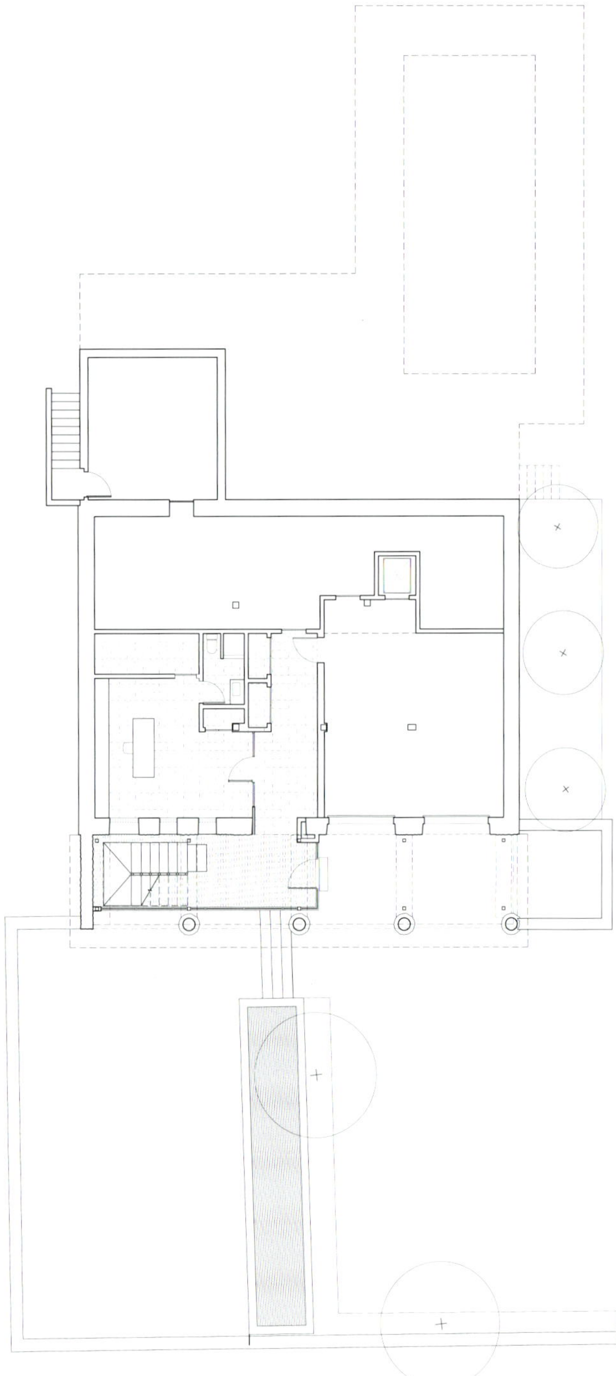

Site Plan

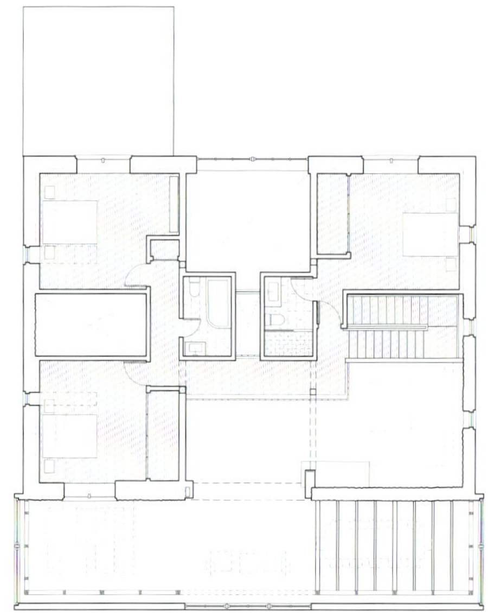

Bedroom Floor Plan

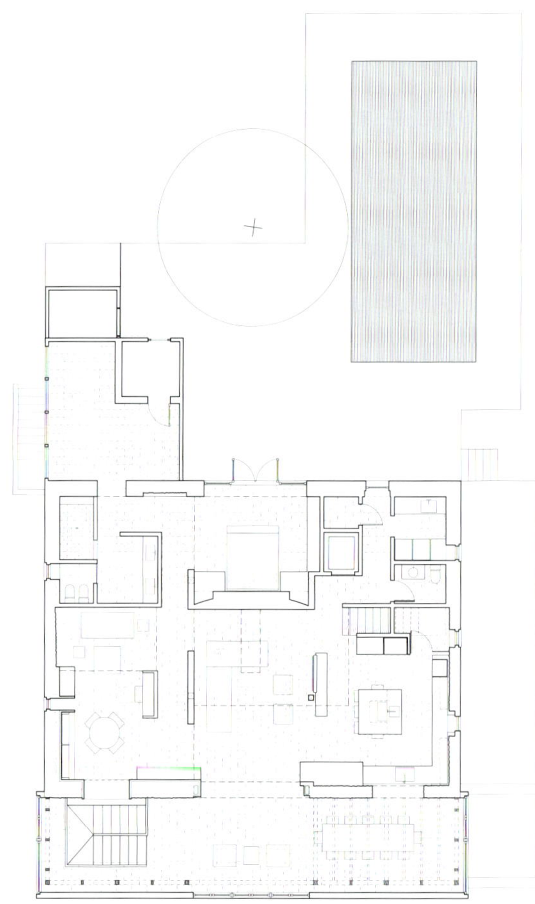

Living Floor Plan

South Elevation

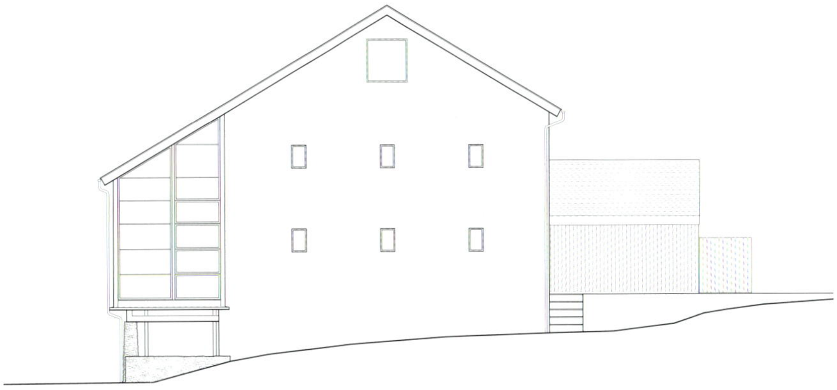

East Elevation

North Elevation

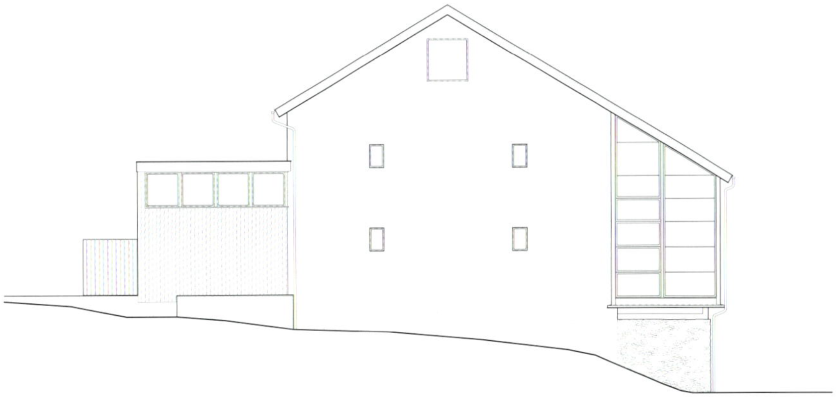

West Elevation

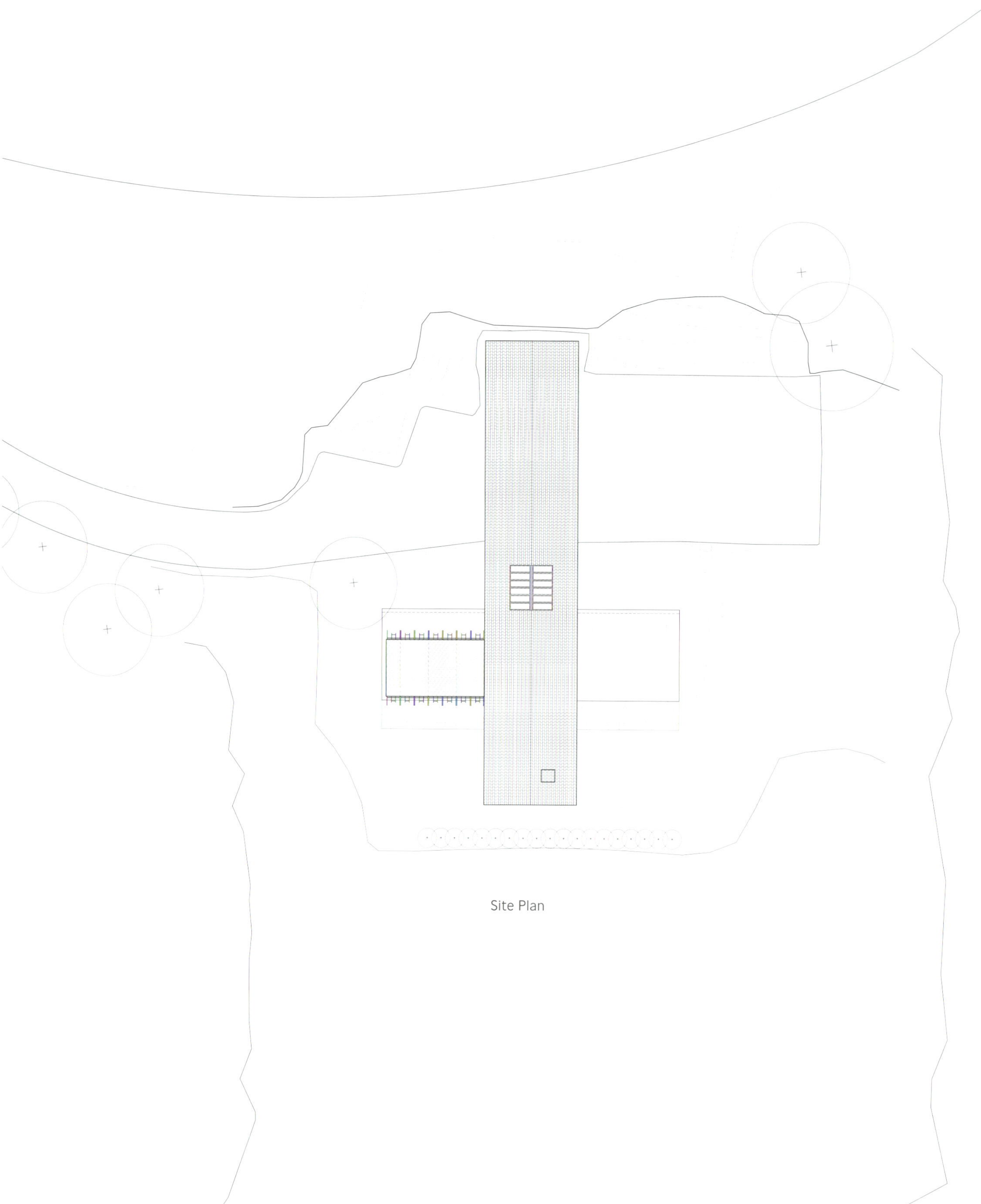

Site Plan

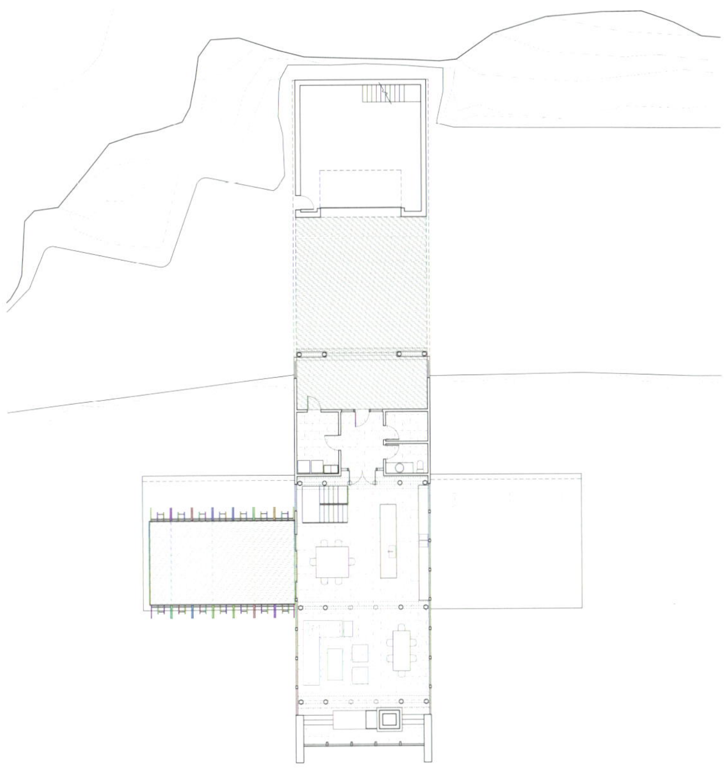

Living Floor Plan

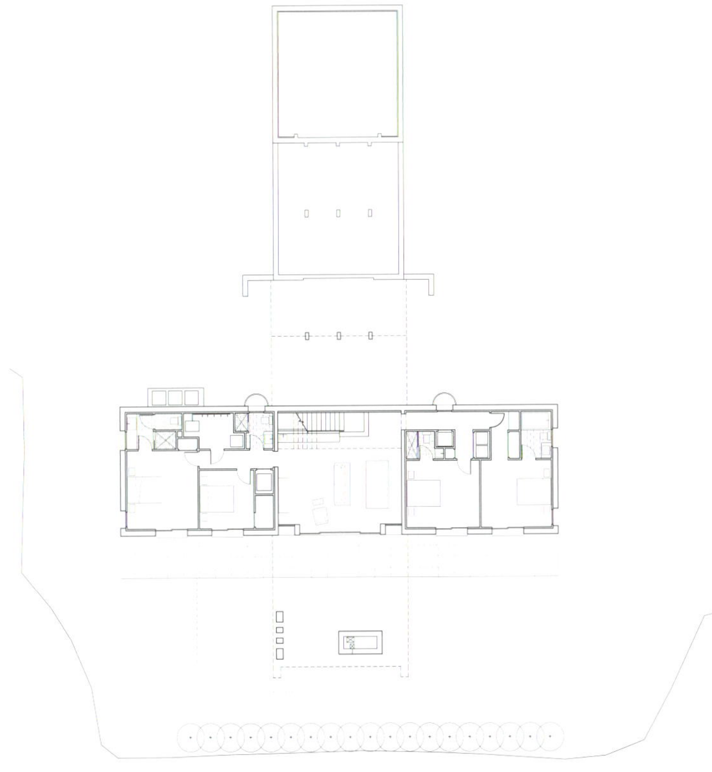

Ground Floor Plan

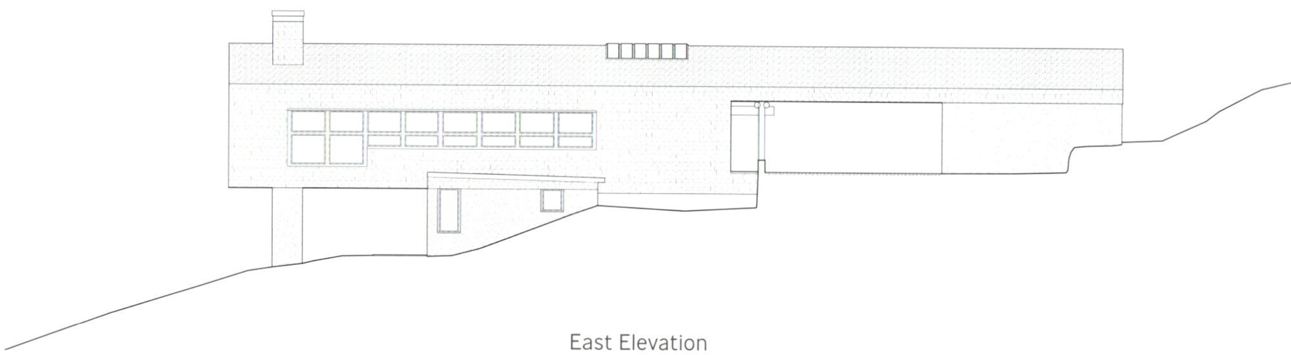

East Elevation

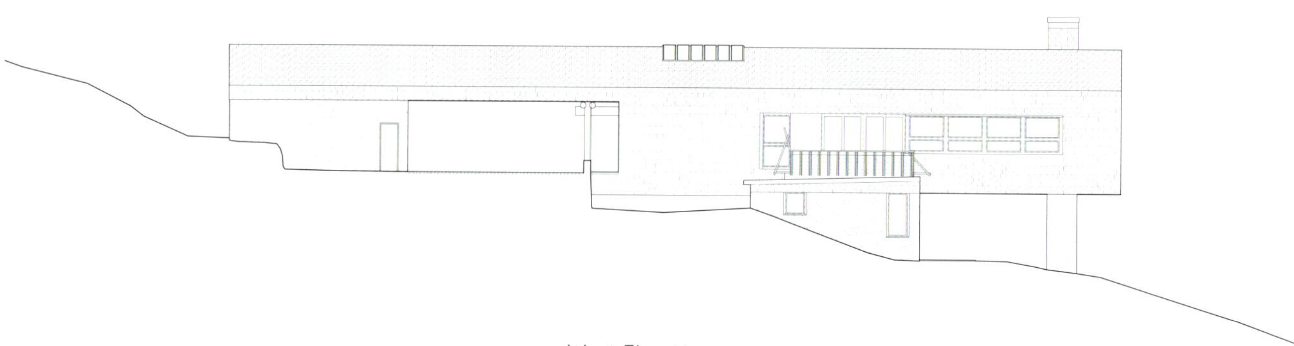

West Elevation

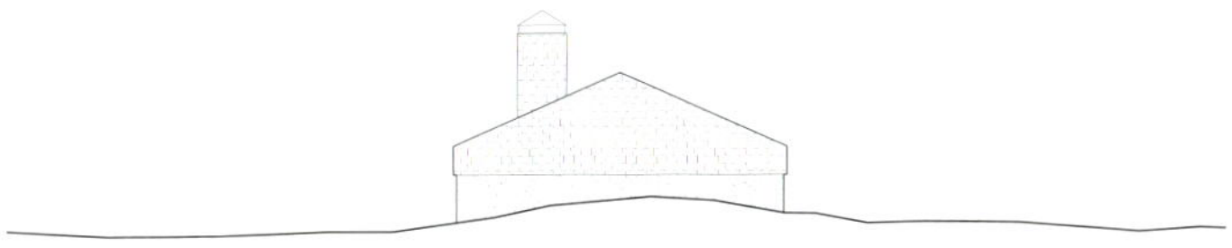

North Elevation

South Elevation

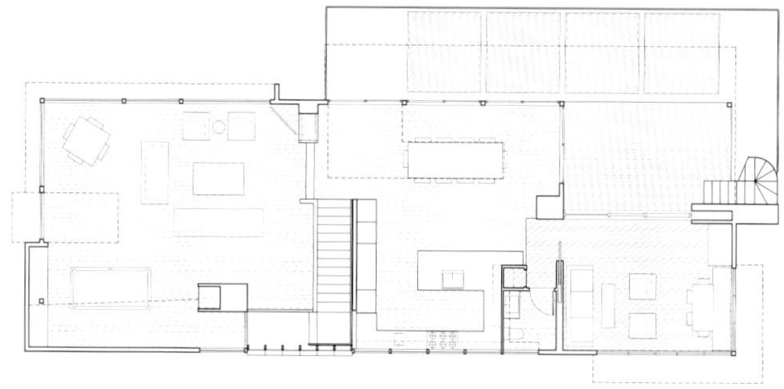

Living Floor Plan

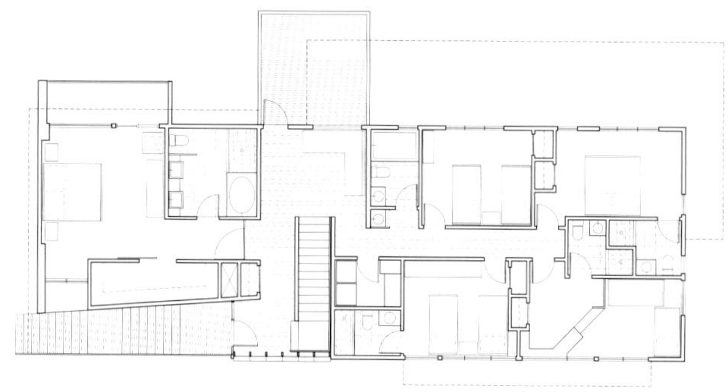

Bedroom Floor Plan

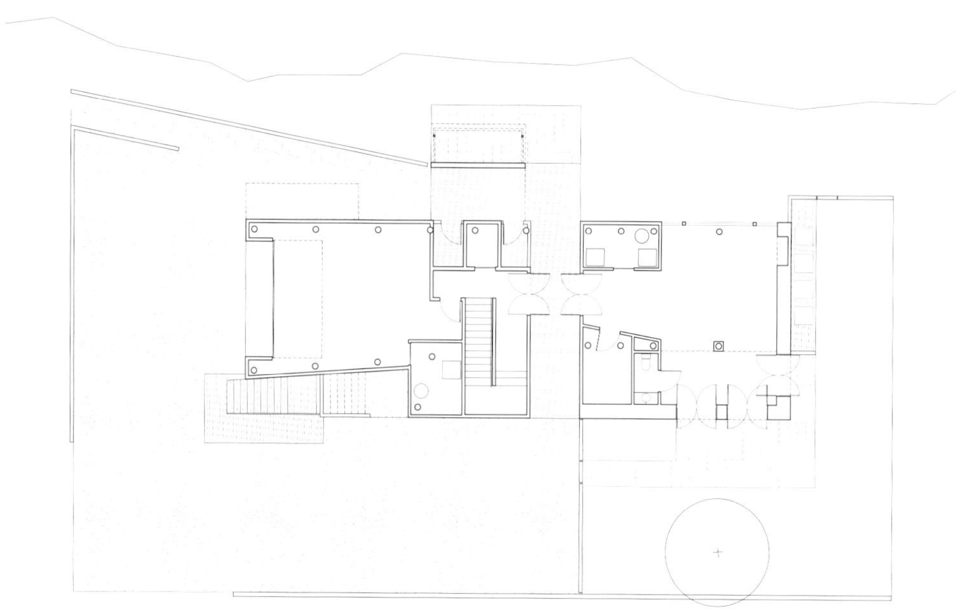

Ground Floor Plan

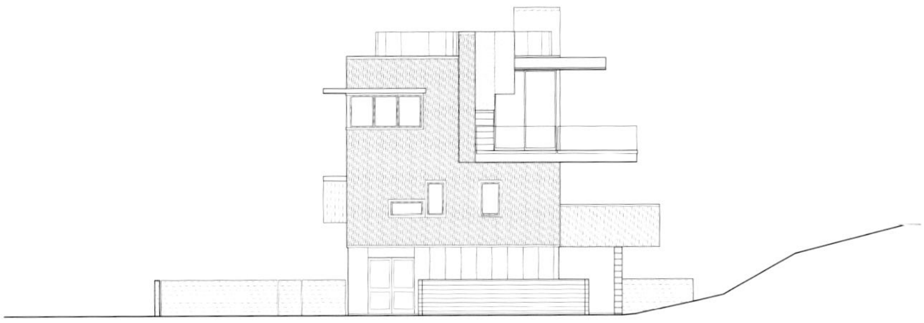

South Elevation

East Elevation

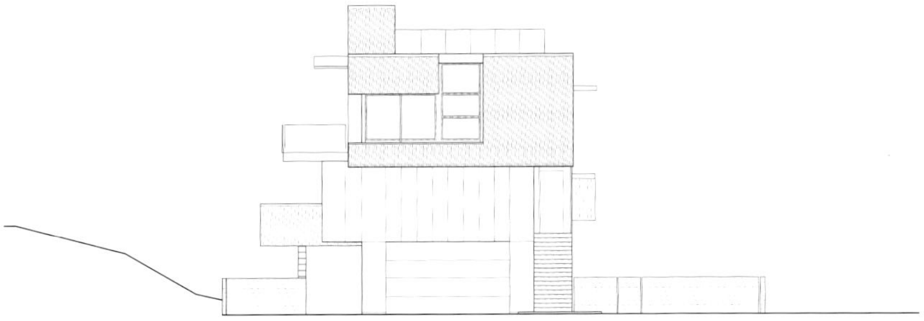

North Elevation

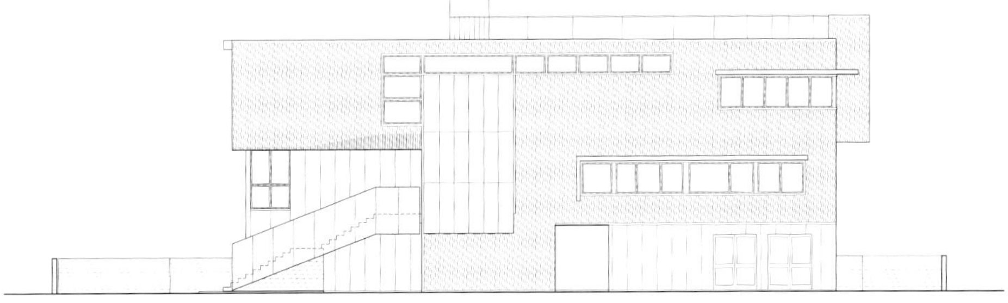

West Elevation

MERCANTILE LIBRARY OF PHILADELPHIA in 1952 immediately after its completion. Closed and vacant since 1989, the building was purchased by Michael Ryan Architects in December of 2011. It will be restored as the Philadelphia office for the firm.

ÖP
KLEIN & GOODMA
CAMERAS
BOLEX
SELF SERVICE
etail Shop

PROJECT CREDITS

BEACH FLOP

Project Team: Michael Ryan, Christopher Jeffrey, Bill Bloomfield, Samuel Kim, Rich Villa
Interior Design Team: Randee Spelkoman, Christopher Jeffrey, Michael Ryan
General Contractor: Harry Wilson Builders
Photographers: ©Paul Warchol, Paul Barnett (Barnett Photographics)

SHEAFF LANE

Project Team: Michael Ryan, Michael Meggitt, Andrew Wilkinson
Interior Design Team: Randee Spelkoman, Michael Ryan, Christopher Jeffrey
General Contractor: C. Raymond Davis & Sons
Photographers: ©Paul Warchol, Catherine Tighe, Herb Engelsberg, Tom Bernard

BAYVIEW

Project Team: Michael Ryan, Jason Birl, Benjamin Galbreath, Samuel Kim
Interior Design Team: Randee Spelkoman, Michael Ryan, Samuel Kim
General Contractor: Gardner Construction
Photographer: Floto + Warner

BARN

Project Team: Michael Ryan, Christopher Jeffrey, Samuel Kim
Interior Design Team: Randee Spelkoman, Christopher Jeffrey, Michael Ryan
General Contractor: Carroll Construction
Photographer: Matt Wargo

BIG INDIAN
Project Team: Michael Ryan, Scott Trombetta, Rich Villa
Interior Design Team: Randee Spelkoman, Michael Ryan, Scott Trombetta
General Contractor: Wolfgang Schlemmer
Photographer: ©Albert Vecerka/Esto

OCEAN RETREAT
Project Team: Michael Ryan, Christopher Jeffrey, Samuel Kim, Rich Villa
Interior Design Team: Randee Spelkoman, Michael Ryan, Christopher Jeffrey
General Contractor: Gardner Construction
Photographer: Barry Halkin

LOGLODGE
General Contractor: Brian Smith Builders
Project Team: Michael Ryan, Michael Meggitt, Anthony Condouris, Martin Montgomery, Michael Mahns
Interior Design Team: Randee Spelkoman, Michael Ryan
Log Structure: Alpine Log Homes
Photographer: Barry Halkin

ROCKY HILL
General Contractor: Brian Smith Builders
Project Team: Michael Ryan, Christopher Jeffrey, Bill Bloomfield, Rich Villa
Interior Design Team: Randee Spelkoman, Michael Ryan, Bill Bloomfield
Photographer: Catherine Tighe

FRENCHTOWN
General Contractor: Brian Smith Builders
Project Team: Michael Ryan, Scott Trombetta, Rich Villa
Interior Design Team: Randee Spelkoman, Michael Ryan, Scott Trombetta
Photographer: Catherine Tighe